There's Always
Hope.

There's Always Hope.

EHSANUL HOQUE

Copyright © 2014 by Ehsanul Hoque.

Interior Illustrations by: Muhtasim Mojnu

Library of Congress Control Number:	2014911662
ISBN: Hardcover	978-1-4990-8755-0
Softcover	978-1-4990-8757-4
eBook	978-1-4990-8756-7

All rights reserved. No part of this book may be reproduced or transmitted in any form or by any means, electronic or mechanical, including photocopying, recording, or by any information storage and retrieval system, without permission in writing from the copyright owner.

This is a work of fiction. Names, characters, places and incidents either are the product of the author's imagination or are used fictitiously, and any resemblance to any actual persons, living or dead, events, or locales is entirely coincidental.

Any people depicted in stock imagery provided by Thinkstock are models, and such images are being used for illustrative purposes only.
Certain stock imagery © Thinkstock.

This book was printed in the United States of America.

Rev. date: 09/12/2014

To order additional copies of this book, contact:
Xlibris LLC
0-800-056-3182
www.xlibrispublishing.co.uk
Orders@xlibrispublishing.co.uk

Contents

Chapter 1	Start of High School	9
Chapter 2	The Parcel	14
Chapter 3	Troubled Alex	19
Chapter 4	Left & Alone	27
Chapter 5	Officially a Crew Member	35
Chapter 6	Bad to Worse	45
Chapter 7	Fire! Fire!	53
Chapter 8	Fresh Start	64
Chapter 9	Trails and Clues	68
Chapter 10	Skill Bout	79
Chapter 11	Worst of all . . .	91
Chapter 12	The Last Days	100
Chapter 13	Expressing Me	103
Chapter 14	Dunkell's High School	107

You have officially opened the book; welcome to the story of my childhood mistakes, troubles, missions, School Drama and lastly success, despite all the problems I've caused. Whilst reading, think from an 11 year olds perspective.

Mind my manners; Greetings, my name is Isaac Ingham. I am 27 years old and currently employed at British Airways as a Co-Pilot. I have been employed with the company since a lucky promotion I had been offered; the company decided to take me on, due to my abundance of skills and qualifications. I haven't written this book for you to know what I do as a career. No. I wrote this as I want you to know how I had struggled to get to this point. I express my past life and how I accomplished in succeeding to become a pilot. Unfortunately, I found no hope, which left me stranded in a mislaid life of misery. The aim I am trying to achieve is to inspire youngsters to think before they act.

I will start off from the beginning, where things began to go wrong in high school. Moving forward, 16 year's ago; I was a trouble maker; a serious trouble maker.

CHAPTER 1

Start of High School.

This is it, the next big step; high school, Moore's East Academy. The majority of my Primary School mates are coming to this school. Luckily, I won't be a loner. First day today so I am looking forward and can't wait to meet new people! Yup, I'm excited especially to see my mates, suited and booted in their new shoes, blazers and ties. This is great! No more SAT'S and tests, just freedom.

Freeze! So as you figured out, I was ecstatic to be in high school, with the cool, big kids and fit girls around me however I had the wrong intention of high school as you're about to find out what mischief I had been up too. Anyway, carrying on with the story . . .

As it is the first day, obviously nothing will go wrong. Incorrect! I got into a fight with one of the older kids at break time. I feel absolutely petrified. I am not sure what I did to provoke him; he comes up to me and shoves me around alongside his other mates. He begins shouting in an angry tone, "Fight me you wimp! Come on!"

Suddenly, someone jumps on me, the lads starts to throw punches. I raise my hands to defend myself and in a matter of seconds, half of the blooming school kids come towards us to see the fight. All I can hear from the crowd is

"Lace him up! Lace him up!"

"Throw another bang!"

"Jab 'im!"

My blood starts to boil and I too start throwing punches at the nutcase opposite me. As wild fists fly round, I knock him down to the floor, get on top of him and endlessly rain down punches. I could not stop. I was out of control.

"INCOMING! MR. EVANS!" bellows a kid.

"Clear off, the lot of you!" shouts a teacher that is heading hurriedly, towards us.

"Oi, get off him!" screams the teacher again. I was still punching this so called 'cool kid' till the teacher decides to rugby-tackle me onto the field. "What is this?! Fighting on school grounds is unacceptable!" He yells.

By now, 7 teachers come from different directions, rushing to see what all the noise is about. Slowly rotating my head around the field, I observe the whole school staring and talking about me. Suddenly, a teacher's face appears straight in front of mine, "What on Earth are you, an animal?! Can't you see what damage you've caused towards another pupil's face?"

I notice the harm that I had committed. The boys features; his nose is bleeding and his left eye has turned purple, also his face looks bloated up. What the heck had I just done? I was too scared to even open my mouth.

We were taken to the Head of Science, Dr. Jameson. The boy was navigated to another classroom to explain what had happened. I was told to do the same. I get handed a pen and paper then told to write. I state: 'I was busy minding my own business and all of a sudden, when the older kid came, he was shoving me. I think it was one of his friends but that person decided to jump on my back. Then, out of nowhere (the boy in the other classroom) start punching me. Afterwards, all I can remember is that I was on top, punching the living daylights out of him. That's when the teacher came and forced me off him'.

That's all I wrote because that is exactly what happened. I gave the statement to Sir. Precisely, 1 hour & 33 minutes later, a rather odd looking man comes into the office. "Are You Isaac Ingham? The teacher said sternly. I mumble "Yes sir, I am."

He sits beside me like he's my friend and gives me a lecture. "Well Isaac, what you've done on your first day here, is horrific! On Transition Day, I have heard that you were a star, putting your hand up for every question, but what happened today?" He was being friendly which I like because he looked quite intimidating, due to his height. I could also see that he is Christian from his bracelet; it is made up of Crosses, the one that Jesus died on."Sir, I honestly don't know. He hit me so I retaliated and I still have no clue why he kicked off with me." He knew the reason why the boy had struck me. "This boy, his names Carlton and he's in Year 9; a real nasty piece of work and from what I have been hearing, he gets his so called 'reputation' by picking on little new kids like yourself." Now I understand why, it became quite clear that Carlton was a vicious being. Sir says "If there are any other issues, come and see me." After, he tells me to go to my next period and not to mention anything to my classmates. I make my way.

Hurrying off, I hear something. It was Carlton trying to communicate with me. "Oi you little runt, Have you any idea what damage you've caused to my face?! Trust me, I'm gonna get you rushed sooner or later!" I had that feeling of panic and fear. Someone walks into the corridor; by the looks of it, it was one of the popular kids that hang's around with Carlton. He comes over and says "Did I just hear you say that you're going to get this youth rushed just because he banged you out?"

Carlton looks down.

"The name's Alex and I've gotta congratulate you for knocking out this muppet who's two years old than you! That's some power you got there lad. Ayy, wanna be part of our Crew?" says Alex, the popular kid. I feel quite shocked. "Seriously, you're gonna get him to be part of Mayhem Crew?" said Carlton surprisingly.

Alex clips him around the ear and tells him to shut it. "Well?" Alex said impatiently.

I struggle to think why they want me to be part of their Crew, but eventually I make up my mind and reply "Okay, cool . . ."

"You've made the correct decision; from now on, you'll chill with me around school and be one of my boys. Now go to lesson and behave yourself. At lunchtime I got a little job for you."

They walk off; I am confused and excited at the same time. He said he has a little job for me and I guess we will find out soon however before discovering what the job is . . . I have no clue where my class is! I see a teacher ahead of me so I decide to ask her. "Miss, I'm in year 7 and don't know of where my class is. Can you tell me where um . . . M7 is please?"

The teacher's young, white, blonde; I'd say she looks quite attractive. "Yes Hun', I'll walk you there now so that you don't get lost again."

"Thank you, miss."

I finally get to the class and all my classmates start praising me as soon as I get in. "OH MY, I HAD NO IDEA YOU COULD FIGHT LIKE THAT!" shouts one of my mates from the back.

"Settle down now, we all have work to do . . ." announces the class teacher.

"What's your name?" She asks me.

I counter, "Its Isaac."

She has a sticky note thing stuck on her cardigan; it reads 'Mrs Barnes.'

"Take a seat just here and I'll be right with you." Everyone is still staring at me. It felt quite awkward but I can't deny the fact it makes me feel prestigious.

CHAPTER 2

The Parcel

The bell rings and everyone starts scattering, trying to get outside the classroom. Its lunchtime and Alex said he has that 'little job' for me, so I head to meet him outside, on the field. While I was walking there, literally everyone was coming up to me to asking why I had a fight with Carlton. I give short snappy answers (all made up) and walk off. In the distance, right at the back of the field, I spot Alex waving; signalling me to come over. As I get closer, I can see that the Crew are lying down like they are hiding. I start sniffing. I can smell the smoke of cigarettes. There are girls and boys mixed, hanging around.

"Yo everyone listen up, this is our new member of our Crew, his names Isaac, Year 7 lad; the one that banged out Carlton." Alex announces.

They all gaze at me like I'm Megan Fox. "Want a smoke?" speaks one of the older kids.

"Nah, I'm cool. I'm a bit too young for that." I respond.

Alex is smoking with the rest of them; there are 6 people; 2 girls and 4 boys, including me. After I meet and greet, Alex calls me over. "So little man, this is our Crew and you're the youngest member; don't worry we'll protect you from any crap that might happen. Anyway it's about that little job I was telling you about earlier. I want you to go and give this parcel to the address written on it after school. Can you do that for me?"

It was a medium-sized parcel and had a street name on top.

"Yep, easy peasy, I'll do it straight away when the bell rings." We slowly drift away from the Crew and he cautiously says "One thing you mustn't do is peak inside it. Just put it in your bag, take it to the address and hand me the money the buyer gives you tomorrow in school. If you do this job successfully, you'll get some money from me. Call it a job, when I need you, you come."

There's nothing hard about this job so I take this parcel from Alex and put it in my bag. We walk back and join the rest.

(The Bell Rings . . .) We have been dismissed; time to go. As soon I get out, I walk towards the toilets. Carefully, I take out the package. The address is '62 Common Road LU9 5BT', it's approximately 7 minutes away from where I'm currently standing. "Isaac?" someone hisses. That shook me!

I am not sure of who it is or what to do.

"Who are you?" I murmur back. I hear footsteps outside this cubicle I'm in.

"It's Alex you doughnut. I saw you get in the toilets so I came to check if everything's alright."

I quickly put the package back in the bag and open the door. Alex is just there, staring directly at me. "Everything's cool man; I came in just to check the address. I'm making my way now." I say.

"You haven't got much time, so leave now and remember, collect the money, go home and give the money to me tomorrow."

Without even saying a reply, I exit the toilets, acting casual and head down the school gates without looking back. I feel so anxious to see what is inside the package so I start thinking what it may be; a gun? The package isn't shaped like one though. Or money? But why would someone want to buy money for money? Maybe it's drugs? I stop thinking about it as it was giving me a headache so instead I give up and carry on walking. At last, I get to 'Common Road' I am on the right side so I cross to the left because the even numbers are opposite from where I am standing. I am looking for No.62 and beside me is No.56; I guess I was nearly there. As I reach the doorstep, I knock on the door. No-one responds, so I knock even louder. After a minute (which seemed like forever) a man opens the door. Immediately I say "I've got a parcel for yah' mate."

"Keep your voice down!" replies the man abruptly. I hand over the parcel and he gives a bundle of cash in return, my eyes lit up due to the amount.

"Now clear off!" orders the ignorant rich man. I stuff the cash in my pocket and head home.

FREEZE! So how many mistakes did I make on the first day of year 7? Well, I had a fight, joined a Crew and delivered a parcel which I had no clue of what was inside. What a great start! Back to the story . . .

I feel happy, calm and untouchable. I have nothing to worry about whilst I am in school because I have got my back up in case I get into any hassle despite the fact that Carlton will be around me most of the time when I am with Alex. Philip knocks for me and we both leave for school (by the way, Philip is my best friend). Whilst we are walking, I tell him all about yesterday; he gives me an apprehensive look and asks me "Do you know what was inside the package?"

He puts me on a point where I respond to him and he screws at me. "No?"

And then he goes bollocks and starts shouting and screaming. I interrupt and tell him "Get to the point . . ."

He replies "It was drugs you idiot!" I feel as if I got kicked in the teeth and was speechless. He changes the subject in a nippy and now we are talking about football. It is as if I didn't even mention about the 'parcel' business to him.

In maths class, I am talking non-stop about different events that happened yesterday (mostly about the fight). The teacher separates us in different parts of the classroom. After the bell rings for second period; the class teacher, tells me to stay behind. "Isaac, this is your second day at this school and you were constantly talking throughout the lesson, however that's not the reason why I've held you back."

"Sorry sir, but what is the reason then?" I ask. He gives me a long stare and responds, "I heard you talk about being part of a Crew to your friends. Out of curiosity, is your 'Crew leader' from this school?"

Here we go again, another question that's left me on point.

"I'm not being rude or anything but what's it to you?" I enquire to the teacher. Sir gives me a demanding look and before he says anything else, I hastily reply yes.

"Thank you, that wasn't very hard, was it? A yes or no question; now, can you tell me he or she's name?" Politely asks Sir; I told him enough so I decide not to say anymore. "I've got to go to second lesson sir, sorry" and quickly rush off.

Why all those questions? Why does he need to know specifically the leaders name (Which is Alex)? I guess I've just given the teacher a clue. Instead of attempting to answer the issue myself, I'd ask Alex if he knows anything about it. Second period is boring, so curiously; I daydream about being a leader of a big ghetto gang. I am soundless throughout the lesson; nevertheless, when the bell rings for break I stand up instantaneously shouting 'FINALLY!' Everyone is staring at me, once again. "Someone's keen to leave, aren't they?" proclaims the teacher. I feel embarrassed so I mutter "Sorry."

Without delay, I run straight towards the back of the field where the crew were yesterday. The same people are here however there is no sight of Alex. "Yo, where's Alex?" I question, so everyone hears me. A guy with curly hair says "He's got detention; he threw a chair at the flabby teacher in H4."

"When's he going to be allowed back out?" I pursue.

"Prob'ly around lunchtime . . ." replies the curly haired boy.

That's great, isn't it? I have to wait another hour to ask him.

CHAPTER 3

Troubled Alex

Our whole year has Modern Foreign Languages (MFL) now. Sluggishly, I make my way to the back of the classroom. "Hola!" excitedly says the Spanish teacher. All the way through the lesson, I stay absolutely quiet however I still put my hands up for several questions. It seems as if I am invisible. No one is talking to me but I can hear people gossiping and mentioning my name.

What are they talking about?

The class are dismissed for lunch and I once again headed towards to the back of the field. Whilst I'm walking 'fast', the maths teacher (the one that is suspicious about the Crew issue) stops me.

Oh no, not again!

"Isaac, I know it's lunchtime but I need to talk to you just for a minute or two. Come in to my classroom." The teacher orders; I trail behind despairingly.

"You said your Crew leader is from this school but can you name the person for me?" asks Sir, again. What am I meant to say? I don't want to be classed as a 'Snitch' if Alex gets into trouble because of me . . . I anxiously come up with a lie from the top of my head,

"Sir, you must promise not to tell anyone."

The teacher promises, pretty much instantly. I decide to tell him, however, not the information he is expecting me to say. "Okay, I'm not really part of a Crew. I made it up so that my friends think I'm cool. Sorry sir."

He gives me a long bewildering glare, "Are you sure?" responds the teacher in an ominous tone; "Yes I am . . ." I reply. I'm still acting as if I am telling the truth and can't wait to tell the Crew that Sir actually fell for it!

"Well then . . . make sure you don't worry me like that again in the future," he says tediously. Immediately I walk off and when I am out of the teacher's sight, I sprint like Usain Bolt down the field, to the Mayhem Crew.

In the distance, I see Alex's bag and shout out his name. He turns his head, seeing me running like a headless chicken and gives me a straight face. As I get there, I try to explain everything that happened. My speech is a blur. A jumble of nonsensical words erupts from my mouth as I desperately attempt to convey the recent confrontation.

"Whoa, slow down there son, take a deep breath and try again," I collapse on the grass, and try to steady my heartbeat, still shaken by the encounter. I stand, and stare Alex directly in the eyes, explaining the situation. Alex stares back, ashen faced and momentarily lost in his own thoughts. Unexpectedly, his lips separate into a huge grin, and affectionately slaps my back, "Great work you did, good lad," responds Alex, I smile back and gratefully accept his praise, "Oh yeah, and the money?" Alex enquires. My hand immediately shoots for my bag, still buzzing from Alex's approval; I rummage for the wad of cash neatly tucked away behind my books. I look about, careful for any curious onlookers; discreetly I place the money in Alex's upturned palm. He takes the money, and divides the cash in two parts, one large portion and another small. Alex then hands me the smaller portion, "Here, there should be a good Hundred Pounds in that," he offers me a sly wink, "Don't spend it all at once mate."

I smile and laugh in return.

The weekends are here and I have nothing else to do, so I decide to call Alex and ask him to meet up. "Sure, meet us in Finsley Park; most of the crew are here, we're planning something and you're in it." casually speaks Alex. I wonder what it is but my mind swiftly drifts away as I reach for my man bag, which has my money and earphones inside, I quickly put on my Nike Air Forces plus my jacket, ready to leave the house. As soon as I shut the door, I feel a cold blustery breeze brush across my face. My body shivers for a second. As I walk, I stop by at the shops to get something to eat, preferably a packet of crisps and a drink. I have £5.25 on me so I have MORE than enough. "£1.25 please," informs the shopkeeper. I reach for my money and take out a fiver. "Cheers and here's your change."

I exit the shop. Approximately, I am four to five minutes away from the crew so I make up my mind and walk promptly as if I am speed walking. I notice that I am looking like a total idiot and getting bizarre looks from pedestrians so I stop and walk like a normal paced human.

"Finally, you're here!" exclaims Alex. It feels so awkward because everyone is looking intently towards me. "Yeah, I stopped by at the shops. Anyway, what's this plan all about Alex?" I proclaim. Assertively, the crew are looking to one another. "Care to explain Mike?" asks Alex. Mike is a big lad, wide and muscular; he has a long jagged scar dragging down the left side of his face. I gaze and think about how that may have happened. Mike interrupts as he begins to speak, "So little man, you know school is so boring and whatnot so we're all planning to bunk for a few days and a couple of periods throughout. So now you understand what we're talking about, I'll move onto the plan . . ." He has a bundle of papers in his hand and gives me one to read. It is printed out and looks proficient; it says:

> *First of all, the individuals that will be bunking on Monday, Wednesday and maybe Thursday; will get together after morning registration outside the Maths block. However you will have to do this vigilantly and attract less attention towards your peers so that they don't find out (especially your teachers or bad news will occur). We will go in groups.*
>
> *Period 1 - 4 people will go.*
> *Period 2 - 5 people will go.*
> *Period 3 - 2 people will go.*
>
> *(You will discuss this amongst yourselves about what time is suitable for you)*
>
> *The remaining left, which will be around 3 to 4 individuals which will make their way between Period 4 and 5. (They will have to figure out which period will be the best to bunk and won't be too bait for the teachers to find out)*
>
> *As soon as you leave the school premises and clearly offsite, congratulations you're bunking class and free for the limited time you have till you got to go back into school for lesson. FOR EVERYONE'S INFORMATION (mainly the amateur bunkers), the bunking exit is at the far, far left side of the field, right at the back. Also, if you are still unsure, don't worry a pro bunker will be with each group, navigating them. Bringing a jacket/coat with a hood is strongly advised*

due to the reason that the teachers cannot spot who you are in case a teacher see's you. Remember to run as fast as you can till you reach the end of the field! If you get given one of these flyers' and are interested in bunking on one of the days, please don't hesitate to see Alex or Isaac for more information. However, if you do get handed a leaflet and drop it by mistake, consequences will take place, so be careful.

Good luck my Certified Bunking Soldiers!'

Seriously, did they have to be THIS prepared just for a few days of bunking? And why's their vocabulary so 'accurate'. Before I ask Alex and the crew why, I noticed my name is included in the 'leaflet' thing. I feel unique, "Alex why did you have to write a whole essay and plan it out step by step?" I ask confusingly.

"Well, this is your first year here; and the amount of people that want to bunk is countless. It's like 'first come first serve' type of thing; they come to you or me to book themselves in, which I will tell you about in a bit. Plus half the people that want to bunk are mostly youngsters and they're still amateur-type bunkers. Besides all of that, are you in or out? You need to answer now" explains Alex; now I understand why but he just asked me a question, am I in or out? This has gone a little too far don't you think? First the fight, then the mystery package (not really a mystery anymore) and now bunking? If I say no, they'll think I'm a coward so without further ado, I casually say 'yes' to Alex. "Okay, now come with me so I can go into depth about this bunking thing so you fully understand what to do and how to do it." Clarifies Alex; I walk off thinking 'Oh great; another mission to be accomplished!'

Weekend's are now over and it is time for school. I wake up, brush my teeth, wash my face, get ready, and quickly eat breakfast and Philip knocks for me. Whilst walking, Philip is nagging on about how Manchester Utd lost the finals. He is boring me to death so I decide to change the subject to the plan about the bunking news however in the last second, I decide not to due to simply because he will have a go at me again. Stupidly, in the last millisecond, I decide to break out the information.

"What the hell is wrong with you? Seriously, you weren't like this in Junior School and I've known you for almost 5 years. Come on man, you're better than this, leave the bad crowd and come back to your old mates. Trust me, truancy will get you nowhere therefore step back and leave it." Advises Philip; I can't believe what he just said; my rage is ready to explode.

"I thought you were my mate? You said you've got my back careless of what I do! Now you're just a hater and a wasteman. This is high school and it's different from Junior's. We meet different people and get along with different kinds! And Alex; He isn't a 'bad influence, he's my friend unlike you, now GET LOST!" I bellow at Philip. He walks off, doesn't look back, he just heads towards another direction. After a few minutes or so, I realise what I had done; I have lost my best friend.

In school, I am not co-operating or taking part in lessons. All I can think about is Philip and how he is feeling. He is probably, confused, hurt and distressed. I guess he was trying to help me but he should not of said things like that to me or the crew (which he thinks is a bad crowd but they are only different types of people; well that's what I think.) Before matters get worse I decide to go find him at break-time and tell Alex I will bunk at Period 4 along with the rest of the leftovers. I have got to sort this out, my best friend comes first. As soon as the bell goes off, indicating break, I head towards the room door and leave. Philip is in the last room down the corridor, I sprint towards his class. Anxiously I wait outside however I don't spot Philip in the room. After the class has been dismissed I ask his class teacher where he is. "Sorry Darling, but he didn't come in today." Responds the teacher; I leave the classroom, puzzled.

Still clueless, I walk towards my next lesson. Whilst strolling, I wonder where he could be. It was my entire fault; if I hadn't shouted at him, he'd probably be in school, making a lot of racket in the corridors. Then a location fired into my brain where Philip may currently be hiding! I think I know his whereabouts! However my mouth turns from a grin to a frown due to the reason that I have to wait another couple of hours till school ends. Just as I'm about get into the class, I remember that I am going to be bunking after lunch with one of the 'senior' bunkers so as soon as I am off site, along with a couple others; I'm going to look for Philip because I think I know where he is. I hope I find him where I assume he's hiding. Every second, I feel guilty and tell myself that it's my intact imperfection.

As I am working efficiently in class, I see Alex looking at me, indicating me to come outside. "Miss, I need to go to the toilet" I say, desperately.

"Hurry up, you've got 2 minutes" replies the teacher. I walk out and Alex immediately says "Why didn't you go and bunk at Period 2 like I told you?" angrily states Alex. He looks fuming. "I err . . . err had to go back for my bag and Sir walked me back!" I instantly reply. He looks a bit calmer now.

"Try not to leave your bag in this class as well because you have to bunk at Period 4, I will too; no excuses!" orders Alex. He saunters off and I enter the classroom. At least he didn't kick me out of the Crew. Anyway, I actually need to bunk at Period 4 to find my missing friend so there is still a positive.

Only 15 minutes left of lesson then I will head over to the crew and ask who is going to bunk with us during lunch. Following that, I will be free and released into a world without school (only for a couple of hours) to do what ever I want.

***FREEZE!** I created another mistake; which was truancy. I'm still part of a Crew and hang around with the wrong surroundings. I've lost my best friend over a pathetic matter. I wish, after I find him that things go back to normal however it wasn't a happy ending. This is where I start doing ridiculous things; it was 'The Start.'*

CHAPTER 4

Left & Alone

As I am walking towards the Maths block; I spot a couple others attentively making their way towards the bunking spot too. As I get there, I see Alex getting ready to make his move. "Wait for me!" I yell. They all look up hurriedly and Alex abruptly whispers "Hurry up!"

We wait for a couple of seconds and unexpectedly Alex is running straight down the field without looking back; the rest follow. As we are running; literally for our lives, we hear a call from behind, "STOP AT ONCE!" barks a teacher from in front of the Maths block doors. It shook us all and increases our pace. We are all huffing and puffing however we are almost there. One by one, we slow down our speed and walk down the bottom of the field.

"That's it, we're clear but one of the teachers spotted us. Let's make our way" speaks Alex, breathlessly. My body is feeling tingly with excitement running through my veins as well as nervousness. I am quite proud however I cannot stop the feelings I'm experiencing. I feel absolutely awesome! After we all capture our breath back, it is time to make the second step; getting under the broken metal fence. One by one, we go beneath the fence. Slowly, I make my move and warily crawl underneath. This is so weird; crawling out of school. Thinking about it like that, almost made me laugh however I held it in, in case I get weird stares from my surrounding peers. As soon I get to the other side, it feels as If I'm in a jungle due to the long crusty trees which darkens my whereabouts. Up above me, I see builders constructing a flat; they did spot us making our bizarre way of getting to the other side. As I am wondering about where I'm standing; Alex is under the fence, almost reaching the opposite side. As he is crawling, one of the builders fiercely tells Alex, (however referring to us also) saying "Oi, get back into the school or I'm going to phone them myself!"

Again there is the feeling of anxiety and I keep regretting doing this in the first place. As soon as Alex crawled out, he shouts "Shut your mouth boldy and get back to decorating!" Immediately, we run along with Alex as we witness the builder getting livid. Finally, we run up this steep hill and when we get to the top, I witness freshly trimmed grass and a park up ahead.

"Come on, let's go." Orders Alex; as we are walking, I'm thinking of a way of getting lost deliberately from the rest because I've got to find Philip. We're strolling around in the park and Alex tells one of the other boy's with us to light up a cigarette. Whilst Alex is smoking and the other two lads join him, I am admiring the view left, right and centre. Everything seems so bright and full of life; I'm attracted.

"Take cover!!" alerts Alex; "Teacher up ahead, Isaac get behind that climbing frame now!" Without delay, I hide behind the frame, crouching, and the other two boy's race towards the bushes. Slowly I slant my head to the right, to check where the teacher is. As I observe the teacher, he is definitely a male and he's incredibly fat.

"Isaac . . . Isaac, use your bag to cover the left side of your face; we're going to make a run to the lamppost which is ahead of us. Sir's still patrolling the park to look for us but we've got to make the move, you enjoying this?" whispers Alex.

Seriously, I've had enough, my body simply cannot hack the amount of adrenaline which is spiralling inside me. However I do have to run with them sooner or later. As soon as Alex told the other two boys the plan, I get my bag ready.

"3 . . .2 . . .1, go" instructs Alex.

Here we go, I'm running as fast as I can till I catch up with Alex; instantly, the teacher pulls out his phone and dials a number whilst witnessing us running; with bags covering our faces. This time, we end up in another park however this one is triple the size of the one before and it's got a golf course with many other activities. All of us put our hands on our kneecaps, catching our breath, once again.

"Too much running for one day" I breathlessly say. Then again, we make off. I'm still thinking of a way to escape from Alex without making it obvious. Instantly I tell Alex "Go ahead, I'm tying my shoelace" He looks at me and nods; at last, a way out.

Without even imagining what Alex will think, I run the opposite direction. I put on my hooded jacket and walk on the main road. Vigilantly, I amble down the path; it was 2:15pm, period 4 is almost over and I've still got to make even with Philip. Philip and I, made this tree-house next to his local park, in the woods when we were in year 5; it has been our chill-out zone ever since we created it and I'm hoping he's there. How will I approach him? What will I say? Forget everything, I'm just going to barge in and say sorry; but what if that's not enough? This will be difficult. I'm

¾ away from our tree-house and I notice my mum driving past. Straight away, I turn around and secrete behind a Vauxhall Corsa. I'm assuming she's coming back from work and hoping she didn't see me; most likely she hadn't because she would've turned around screeching her tires against the road and wouldn't look back to witness the other driver's reactions due to her risky action; my mum would do that, she says she cares about me but the more she get's over protective, the more it annoys me.

After all of today's bizarre moments, I'm looking forward to reunite with my best friend however there is a slight twist. There is no tree-house no more; it has been destroyed! Shockingly, I walk towards the wrecked pile of wood. I couldn't believe it, who could've of done this? Nevertheless it only took a couple of seconds to figure out it was the one and only Philip. Something caught my eye; it is a piece of lined paper neatly folded on top of the wood discreetly tucked in between. I open it; it said:

Dear Best Friend,

We've had our ups and downs but we've always managed to pull ourselves back together. We've been through a lot mutually and have unforgettable memories. I didn't know how to write this to you but my dad found a new job in Australia. Sadly, the whole family has to move too, including me which means you won't see me no more. I couldn't find a way to tell you every time we walked to school but today when you shouted at me, I couldn't cope with the pressure/stress so I decided to lash my anger out on the tree-house because everything seemed so unfair! I'm sorry for destroying it but if I'm not here to hang around with you, then I don't want it to exist and you to have memories of us two every time you chill out there. It'll make you more upset. By the way, inside my school locker is a surprise for you but you know that I can't keep a secret so I'll tell you what's in it; it's my life savings so far that I have collected and precisely there is £100.27 inside the box. You will always stay my best friend and I will never forget you. Even if I'm on the other side of the world, doesn't mean we can't communicate; we'll talk on Skype every day. I'm leaving today in the evening so if you're not angry with me no more, come round my house and say goodbye. I'm going to pack up soon and head to the airport.

P.S. On the back of this letter is a picture of us two so you don't forget how strong our friendship was and obviously how I look like lol.

The tears are rushing down my cheeks and guilt is all I could think about. If I hadn't talked non stop about my school life, he could've had the chance to tell me what was going to happen. This is all too much of a shock so I decide to quickly flip to the other side of the paper and observe the picture of Philip & me on the Year 6 end of year trip to Thorpe Park. I put the letter in my back pocket and head for his house. My eyes are red and overall my face is gloomy. I start to walk out of the forest thinking about the future and how weird it's going to be when he's not around. Up ahead is his house but I take my time and walk. Usually I take the pedestrian path as a normal person would do, however because of the bolt from the blue news; I didn't realise I was walking on the grass, ruining my school shoes. I step on his doorstep and knock incredibly slowly. It took a few minutes till Philip's dad opens the door "Isaac. Come in." Says Phillip's dad, surprisingly. Disheartened, I enter; my head looking down towards the marbled floor. "Isaac!" Calls Philip; my head rotates as quickly as lightning towards Philip's direction. He was standing on the stairs; I feel content after seeing Philip so I rush towards him and give him, what we call a bear hug. Apologetically, I repeat 'sorry' for 100 times for shouting at Philip. "It's alright man" calmly replies Philip. We walk towards his bedroom as we have lots to talk about.

"Sorry that I didn't tell you any earlier but I couldn't find a way to tell you; even writing the letter, I struggled" apologetically says Philip.

My head slants slightly forward towards Philips direction; I couldn't move my mouth;

He continues talking. "Even though we won't be face to face, we can Skype each other everyday. I know you're shocked but I still am too." He reaches something from inside his inner blazer pocket. "I know that I gave you some money already" (I completely forgot about that!)

"But there's something else I'd like to give you; it's my IPod and my Match Attacks Cards."

My eyes light up due to the things he is giving me, first of all, his IPod; that meant the world to him, he would carry it everywhere. Then there is his Match Attacks, he has some of the most greatest football players included in his deck; I can't believe that he'll give it away.

"Philip, the money is enough and I don't even need that either, what is all this man? These are your things so you keep them" I explain. He doesn't look too shocked however seems down-hearted.

"Come on brother. You need something of mine so that you don't forget me, so just take it as a gift" responds Philip.

"Bruv', I don't need your things to remember you by, you will always be my best friend and your items won't help me remember you; my heart will always tell me because you are part of it. Blood Brother's for life yeah?" I clarify.

We both start to tear up so immediately we stop and give each other a big hug. We connect our knuckles together and repeat jointly 'Blood Brothers.' We get up and I start to help Philip to pack. He has already packed one suitcase so I help him with the next one. Whilst packing up we talk through our memories, up and down moments.

I reach for his clothes from the wardrobe and neatly place it in the suitcase. How is this possible? My mind cannot still work out how I will cope without Philip; we went through too much together for it all to collapse at this stage of life. But I guess sometimes life isn't fair. My best friend will become my no friend.

After a couple of hours, everything is finalized; we all end up at the doorstep. Philip's family and I; this is it I guess.

"Isaac, thank you for being such a loyal friend to Philip" states Philip's dad; he gives me a handshake. His mother nods her head too. I look up to Philip and hug him rigidly.

"Are you trying to kill me with the hugs?" pants Philip.

"Sorry bro, have a good future and hopefully I'll come visit one day" I notify.

"Yep, definitely come visit and if my parents agree; we'll come visit too" replies Philip.

"Time to go then Philip" proclaims Philip's dad. I give Philip one last, and once again our knuckles connect and we repeat 'Blood Brothers'. Tears are starting to pour out, and before they do, I walk out rapidly; don't even look back. Sobbingly, I exit his street.

CHAPTER 5

Officially a Crew Member

The next morning; I yawn loudly and get out of bed. Normal routine I proceed to get ready for school however before I left the house, my mood saddens as there is no 'friend' to walk with. All alone, I walk the cold silent streets and take the usual path; normally Philip and I race up the hill but today I stroll sluggishly up the hardened mud. As soon as I reach the top, my mood lightens a bit when a memory comes to my head when Philip & I used to do 'Knock Knock Ginger' to houses in this area. A memory jolts to my mind, I remember this time when Philip had to go knock on a door on my left, and just as he was about to knock, a massive guy that had a tattoo covering his whole arm came out and gave Philip a daunting stare; I've got to say, it did scare me too even if I wasn't in Philip's position.

Then what happened was the man gripped Philip by his shirt and said "what are you doing on my door step?!" It was a funny moment but Philip was soundless like his lips were glued together; he was stuttering as the words could not come out of his mouth. Forcefully the man pushed him away and ordered him never to step in front of his door again. After being released, he literally ran for his life; when he had got to me, I could not stop laughing! What a memory!

Thinking about that, I didn't realise that I am now in the woods path; this place is quite creepy and I have got to admit that, it is a little scary without Philip by my side. I stop thinking about Philip plus the woods and visualize about what I am going to say to the Mayhem Crew about where I was yesterday. I can't simply say that I got lost because then they would've expected me to go to 'home' (the area where we all meet up.) Gradually, an excuse pops up in my head. I'll just say,

"Alex, while I was tying my shoelaces, I spotted one of our teachers; it was that bold, huge PE teacher! Before, I could catch up with you lot, I quickly turned the other way to duck so that it wouldn't attract any attention; that's why I got separated from you lot!" However I'll say this in an exaggerating manner so it makes it a bit more believable.

I'm en route to school and spot a couple of boys from my year so I chase up to the boys' and walk with them. We greet each other and stroll to school. Several minutes later when we stop by at the shops, I have £2 on me so I go in as well and buy an energy drink as alongside a Snickers bar. Then off we go again, heading to school. Our school is multicultural which I like because we can interact with different people from different backgrounds. Up ahead, I notice Carlton with a few lads, smoking behind the bushes. I panic inside as I try to figure out how to avoid the boys. "One sec, I forgot to get something from the shop" I mention to the people I am walking with. "Ok, cool" responds one of them. As soon as the boys in my year cross the road, I take a left and head towards another direction en route school. Cautiously, I keep my eye on Carlton just in case if he spots me. Luckily, he doesn't so I sprint down the road and take a quick right at the zebra crossing and walk casually down the school road.

Finally, after I get into the school building, I walk straight towards my form room because I really cannot be bothered to go see Alex. Unfortunately, Alex is suspiciously standing outside the library (my form class); when he see's me, he walks forward. "Where did you end up yesterday?" warily asks Alex. Without hesitation, I explain the 'white' lie. He gives me a mystifying look and responds "Fair enough", without further delay, he walks off; doesn't even look back. Phew! That was quite scary! The bell rings the second time notifying us that students must now make their way to their form rooms. Miss tells us to come in and sit down. Majority people look sleepy; I am a bit as well.

"Hello Fable 8, how are you lot feeling?" no-one responds. "I'll take that as tired then shall I? Besides that, I have received an important email from the Attendance office. There were a number of students that truanted yesterday; 3 people have been caught but the teacher's are on the case." Straight away, this caught my attention; my eyes flew up paying attention to every word that is coming out of the teacher's mouth. She continued "If someone knows anyone that wasn't in class yesterday when they should have been, please report it to me." Oh my days! Teachers' have already realised students bunking; I definitely took a major risk yesterday but anyhow it felt good because at least I got to see my best friend before he left right? Later on, Miss goes on to other information and notices such as: attendance record, sports curriculum etc. In the last five minutes, all the year 7's (which includes me) have to go and sit besides Miss's desk. "So year 7's, how are you finding this school so far?" politely says our form tutor. Individually, we say our opinions; Miss is taking down notes. Afterwards, she asks what the pros and cons are of the teachers teaching in the school. Then again she takes down notes as year 7 students fling answers at her.

After she collects all the information that she got out from us, eventually the bell rings, telling us its time for first lesson; I have PE.

We all casually leave through the double doors and make our way into different directions losing one another due to the bigger kids walking through the corridors budging us and not giving a damn, I catch up with a boy in my classes and walk with him towards the changing rooms.

The weather is looking absolutely fantastic! I feel calm and chilled, as there is not any bother with the climate conditions. As I carelessly walk into the changing rooms, I see a group of boys gathering on another lad. I am cautious so I ask a guy next me what is happening. He looks and sees if he recognises me; then he offers me a handshake. In return I slide my hand into his and we shake. "You see the boy sitting down? Well he is about to fight that guy opposite from where I'm standing." I turn my head around and spot a bulky guy rubbing his knuckles; I shiver with fear. What is his opponent thinking? He looks as skinny as a stick but I have heard a few things about him like he can fight even if he's thin. Anyway, I am looking forward to this! Fighting entertainment, I like. Quickly we all get into our parts of the room where we will change whilst the two boys get together, they depart a few steps from each other and stance their positions. I am in the corner of the room and can witness the whole fight without anyone in front of me. Someone from the changing room shouts "Fight!" The boys circulate, and wait for one to throw the first punch; this is heart-beating. Out of nowhere, the big guy rugby tackles the skinny one and drops him onto the floor. Loud, odd noises are coming from the lads standing around expressing the pain the skinny boy which he would have been feeling. Now the two boys are throwing punches at one another careless of accuracy. All the boys are hyping and making way too much noise; a teacher is sooner or later to enter the changing rooms. I quickly signal one of the boys to hold onto the door as I am sunk into the fight; not allowing myself to take my eyeballs off of it. They both roll onto one another and everything really became a blur. Shockingly, the skinny boy is on top punching the big guy rapidly, continuously cursing and blinding. I noticed that no one is going to stop the fight. I immediately think to put an end to it as I observe the big boy looking as if he is going to lose his consciousness.

Without thinking properly, I dive like an American football player and grip the skinny boy, repeatedly telling him that he has won. He calms down and lads rush to congratulate him. The big boy gets up looking extremely hurt; he sits down holding onto his head. At this point, the teacher enters the changing rooms; right away everyone rushes to their hooks and tries to act normal. This made me want to laugh to see how much of a wimp these guys really are. "Boys, hurry up! Half of you aren't even changed! I'll give you 30 seconds and the remaining will do 30 press-ups! Don't waste my time!" Bellows Mr. Ray, the sports teacher.

We all scurry to get changed into our kit. As soon as the sports teacher left, the talking began. Everyone was talking to the skinny guy, not even acknowledging to the big lad. As soon as I wear my tracksuit bottoms, I feel a bit down-hearted for the big lad so decide to go speak to him. "Yo, you win some and you lose some, it's no biggy." He doesn't even look up, just slowly gets changed. No response so I walk off. I am about to open the door when the skinny boy grips onto my arm "Thanks for stopping it or seriously I would have killed him". I look at him and tell him not to worry, open the door and exit. By the time we all get out of the changing rooms, we all forget about the fight. "Everyone make your way to the Astro Turf; we will be doing Football. A slight cheer is raised however the

PE teacher ignores it. In a matter of seconds, we all race up to the Astro. "2 laps of the Astro!" shouts the teacher from a distance. People start sprinting like dogs, including me. Above, I can see the clouds closing up, clashing into each other. A sign of rain is what I think; my mood depends on the weather, weird right? Anyhow, the majority of us did our laps and are panting non-stop. "Terrible fitness" says the teacher. We all attempt our best to stop panting at this rate as we try to stand out to the teacher. The teacher orders us to get into groups of 6. After that, another group and we are navigated into different pitches; we are at the far-end. We all get into positions and I'm told to play in the left wing, I do as I am told by another boy that thinks he is 'captain'. After positioning everyone the teacher blows the whistle, the game begins. Another PE teacher rolls a ball onto the pitch and we run to the ball. We pass it around continuously till we reach their half. The ball comes to me and someone shouts out 'Run!' I find myself running pace fully; another instruction is shouted out "Shoot!" My brain says shoot right away however I tell myself to find aim and to go a bit closer. I slow down, and lean back ready to take the shot. I release and toss my leg full speed. Suddenly, one of the defenders, dives in the way blocked the shot with his right calf. Well, that is a complete waste! "I said shoot earlier!" screws the so called 'captain' of our team. I turn around and give him the biggest dirtiest look. He notices the look and seems a bit fearful. The keeper blasts the ball down and our defenders try clearing it; they are successful.

***FREEZE!** Before I carry on with the story, I'd like to move on. So forget the PE session and let's go onto break time. (Time-machine!)*

At break time, I rush over to the cafeteria to grab a drink. Whilst I desperately rush over due to dehydration, Alex puts his arm around me and takes me to the opposite direction. Oh no! Why now?! "I've got a little job that needs doing" he says. "You see that Polish boy over there?" (He points straight at him) "Well, you and a few others are going to give him something that he deserves; he hasn't been a very good boy so I'd like you to beat him up for me!" My minds quite confused however I agree to do it as long as I am not alone whilst I commit the act. He handshakes me and says "At lunchtime, outside the ICT block" and drifts away. I think about it for a bit and then rush over to get a drink. I just make it in time to buy one; phew! I take a big slurp of the orange juice and walk to Drama. Nothing's better than an orange juice on a hot summer's day!

Drama is a good lesson; I enjoy it. Today we have to put a piece of performance together expressing a horror scene. Whilst we are rehearsing, I see the polish boy that I'm meant to help beat up. He is quite small and looks like a lightweight so I guess the job wouldn't be too hard. Was I sure that I wanted to do this? Of course! 100%! Only because you get to beat up someone for the fun of it plus you get reputation and get recognised for doing it, it's a way for your peers to think that you're strong. I'd probably lay the first punch as I have acquired recognition from beating up Carlton. I wonder how the boy will feel after we knock him out, but that doesn't matter. Let's get this next job over and done with. Later on, it is our go to perform the horror piece; I play the murderer who chainsaw's the innocent victims that enter the haunted house. As the lights narrow down to the centre of the room where our characters are standing, we get into position. The scary background, doll screaming instrumental plays; the drama piece starts. I am behind the curtains ready to creep up behind the daring college kids, preparing to chainsaw their necks in! Blood, guts and gory, sounds scary; I peek through the curtains and witness our class, not moving an eye off the performance. 3, 2, 1 . . . BOO! I jump out and chainsaw the first sufferer whilst the class scream with horror and start laughing; this is incredible acting! After I did all my other cold-blooded murders, the play ends with the college kids which reincarnate and repeat together 'You're next!!' You can see the fear on the pupils' faces' plus the teacher. We end our performance with a bow and face up to a huge round of applause. The teacher states our highlights of the performance and mentions our individual efforts. "A fantastic actor that gets away with murder!" says the Drama teacher. I feel really proud and also hyped up; I'm definitely up to beat the crap into this low-life Polish boy!

Alex said the rest of the boys' are outside the ICT block so I head down there. Casually walking, I see Alex, and he nods at me; I nod back and he figures out that I am going to the ICT block. When I get there, one of the lads tells me to lay the first punch; there's no surprise in doing that. He explains to me to make up a story and hit the guy. "He's coming!" whispers a boy. Everyone rushes into little hiding positions and I just stand there, clueless. The Polish boy looks at me, suspiciously. I stare back. "Remember what I told you!" murmurs the boy that told me what to say. I take in what the lad said; the Polish boy tries to walk past me however I step on the left and block his way, he tries to go and exit onto the opposite direction however I step in front of his view once again. I think this guy's in Year 8 because I saw a few other boys in his year leave from the same class room. Luckily, he is just a bit taller than me. I grip him by his blazer and say the following "I heard you were spreading rumours about me, is that true?!" The Polish boy looks shocked so without delay I punch him right onto his right cheek bone. As he goes down to hold the pain in, the rest of the lads' come and demolish him, completely. I join in to and stomp on him a few times; the Polish boy is grunting louder and louder!

We hear a door open, a few classrooms back so we run out onto the field, laughing and smiling, and the adrenaline rush feels so good! We run right to the back of the field, Alex is there. "Well. Well is the job complete?" Alex says.

"Mate, complete isn't even the right word Bruv!" proclaims one of the boys' who attacked the Polish boy with me; we all handshake each other in order of achievement. Afterwards, I realise that the boys' that knocked out the Polish boy are part of the Mayhem Crew; they light up a couple of cigarettes, the boys' release a sigh of relief. "C'mon Isaac, have a pull . . ." speaks Alex. I am not really sure however because I feel left out and excited, I tell Alex I'll do it but he would have to tell me how to do it first. "It's easy! Make your lips into a circular shape and suck onto the bud but don't do it too fast or you will start to cough. Once it's in your mouth, inhale it like you're taking a deep breath and then release the smoke. It's simple!" Everyone around is staring at me which put a little pressure onto me.

Alex offers the lighted cigarette, slowly I reach out for it, securing the cigarette tightly, pressing it with my thumb and index finger. Next step is to take it in, I eye the cigarette up for a couple of seconds and then closing my eyes, I place it onto my lips and follow the steps Alex told me to do. I take in a large inhale and release. I think like I am one of the big boys now, feeling free. "See, a natural smoker!" declares Alex. The rest of the Mayhem Crew, High Five me with respect; I smile in return. I return the cigarette back to Alex but he refuses and tells me to smoke it. I do so. "So, what should our next missions be?" questions the Mayhem Crew "any ideas?" I think for a while and then respond to Alex "Well, I have an idea in mind. Let's make our own smoke bomb and let it off in school tomorrow lunchtime."

He looks at the grass and then says "okay, we will do that but first of all, how do you make your *own* smoke bomb?" The crew are also taking interest to this bizarre idea of mine. I explain to them; "first you get a table tennis ball, second you spray deodorant onto the ball, third you wrap the table tennis ball in foil, after you light all around the ball till it becomes a ball of fire which you then quickly chuck onto the floor and step on it. Then so much smoke will come out of the ball. I'm telling you, it'll be wicked!" Everyone is literally just staring. Finally Alex responds "okay then big man, YOU will do this alone, and we will test your braveness but don't worry we will support you while you do your business." I imagine what will happen and the imagination I come across makes me more determined. "Ok, fine I will do it alone" I reply.

CHAPTER 6

Bad to Worse

The next day I prepare for this 'smoke bomb' plan that I plan to do. Before I leave for school, I quickly get two table tennis balls (in case the first one fails), grab a Lynx deodorant and then go in to the kitchen to get some foil. Mum and dad are asleep so I can do this without them getting suspicious. However, just as I am getting organized, my sister decides to come downstairs and eat breakfast. (By the way, she also goes to the same school as me but she is in year 10, 3 years older) luckily she hasn't heard about the trouble I have done or been involved in just yet except the fight that I got involved in; apart from that, she thinks I am a good little angel, which is awesome due to the things I've done so far! "What you doing?" says the sister.

"None of your business" I instantly respond. Casually I walk off before she replies. I run up to the upstairs toilet and carry on with my smoke bomb. Oh my days! Just as I am about to enter the toilet, my mum decides to wake up and enter the toilet. "Morning Isaac" greets Mum, yawning. I give her a smile back and nip downstairs again; I would do this in my room but it is quite obvious due to the racket of the foil and smell of deodorant; it will attract attention, and that is one thing I will need to avoid.

This time, I go to the downstairs toilet, hoping no one will be inside. I see no sign of my sister, hoping she wouldn't be inside so I have an attempt to open the door. Guess what? My sister's in this toilet! I quietly moan with frustration. Finally I give up and simply walk out of the house. I take the usual route to school, up the scary, druggy hill, down the car park and through the flats, however I quickly stop before I exit through the flat doors. I pull out the table tennis ball, tin-foil and deodorant. I sat onto the flat stairs, place the equipment beside me. Firstly, I get the ball, firmly gripping onto it. Then, I get the spray and scatter the deodorant out; it smelt nice. After the ball is drenched with deodorant, I grab the tin-foil and carefully wrap it around the ball making sure the foil does not rip. Finally, I screw the bottom of the foil, rotating it so that the foil does not come undone however I repeat the process due to the first one may be a failure. After a good three minutes, I stand up. I hear a door open a floor above me; startled, I open the entrance in front and walk out. I continue my journey to school, all I need is a lighter (which I can get off the Mayhem Crew) and also some nerves because right now, I am quite frightened.

Towards my left, I see a couple of members from the Mayhem Crew; they are one year above me. "Safe" I greet. They handshake me and one of the boys asks me "so you're pull off your smoke bomb stunt today right?"

Jumpily, I reply "obviously! I can't wait you know, to see everyone's reaction!" They give me a proud-like smile. Another lad lights up a cigarette then passes the cigarette deck to the other boys. They each take one out and light it up. "Want one?" questions a boy. I am not really sure but I had one yesterday so I also take one out of the deck; the boy lights it up for me. Wow! A big impact when I take the first puff! A shot-like that directly hit my throat! "Beginner right?" asks a lad.

"Yeah man, this is quite strong!" I respond. My eyes begin to clinch.

"You're a better beginner than me though; when I first started I couldn't stop choking!" He says. One of the boys butts in and speaks "That was hilarious!" I continue to puff on to the given cigarette. I have a head rush. "I feel light-headed though man" I announce.

They look at me, smiling. "It happens, you're not hooked onto it yet that's why." One of the boys respond. I sense tiredness.

We stop by at the row of shops; I have not ever been this way to school before so I am examining my surroundings. The boys I am with; there are three of them, two go into the shop and one goes to the milkman. Why? It seems quite ridiculous. Probably it is his relative or something. I then notice him handing the milkman over some change, the milk man walks into the shop. The two boys I am with come out with four 35p energy drinks with them. The boy offers me a drink, I take one. A minute later, the milkman appears again; he hands over loose change and a deck of cigarettes to the other lad I'm walking with. So I see, their very own supplier; a milkman. It is quite ridiculous you know, this guy can lose his job but oh well at least we're getting what we need.

All three of us then go to the lad with the cigarettes, we continue walking. I casually ask 'the boy with the deck' his name. "It's Callum." He says. Callum opens the fresh deck and hands the other two boys another cigarette each. He then offers me one but this time I reject it because I don't think I can cope with more tiredness; however slowly I do start to get excited. I am now jumpy and trying to liven up the walk towards school.

Stupidly, I run up to this door on my left and knock abruptly which leads to us boys running down the road. "What is wrong with you, you joker" says Callum. I didn't really know.

I laugh and say "I have no clue but I'm feeling so hyper right now!" They grin and stand behind a bush, finishing their cigarettes off. "How do you cope smoking that much cigarettes in the morning?" I question. Callum answers "Used to it and don't call them cigarettes, we call them Snouts so it is less obvious." I take in what he says and Snouts, I like the sound of that.

They each stamp onto their cigarette, one of the boys pull out chewing gum and they pass it around. After that, Callum reaches into his bag to get deodorant; they release the spray onto their finger tips and onto their clothes. I do the same also. "We do this to make it less obvious, you get me?" Callum tells me. As we get in, we walk and make our ways to different directions. We handshake each other and disappear. I head towards the cafeteria; normally my year and the Crew are there. Several boys from year 7 are at the back so I walk towards them. Unexpectedly, this lanky guy appears in front of me. "You're Isaac right? Yeah, so I've heard that you're going to let off a smoke bomb, that's nuts man! Where you going to do it and let me quickly see it?" It takes me a bit of time to take in what he has said. I speak out "yeah, I ain't sure where to do it, probably on the field." I dig into my pockets and wiggle my fingers trying to get the table tennis/smoke bomb out. "Here" I give it to him. He examines the foil that lies round the ball, a good couple of seconds later; he says "Impressive." He gives it back and offers a handshake.

After returning a handshake back I continue to walk to my friends. When I get there, I notice how different students that came from different primary schools, hanging around together as if they have known each other for a long period of time. "Safe lads" I proclaim. They greet me back. They are talking about football, as usual. Few minutes later, the bell rings for form time. We all put on our bags and walk into different directions. In Form, we are watching News-round, it is very interesting. We youngsters hardly even watch the news however News-round gives us an insight to the ongoing life around us. 2 minutes with a lot of information that we enjoy, which is why I prefer it. Everyone is so into the video, one of the headlines is about Jimmy Saville 'the rapist'. A boy in our Form is making jokes about Jimmy. I would prefer not to mention them. The Form Tutor stops the clip due to the immature comments the boy is making behind me. "Thank you for that Marcus, now we are not even going to watch it" proclaims the teacher. Marcus gives a childish grin back. What an idiot.

FREEZE! *I will skip to the Smoke Bomb action because there was nothing interesting about the first two lessons.*

Nerves are slowly taking over; my palms are sweating as well as the top of my head. Gradually, a few boys from the Mayhem Crew gathered round. We are waiting for Alex to meet us at the back of the field. I get the balls out and place them into my blazer pocket. I fiddle around with them. "So you're ready yeah? This is going to attract a lot of attention so if it does work, leg it" speaks one of the lads that's gathered around. Two other boys nod their head, agreeing. The boys light up a cigarette and pass it around between them. A couple minutes later, I see Alex walking towards us. Immediately, I get out the table tennis ball and screw the tip of the foil once again. Behind Alex, another two boys are with him. Straight away Alex hands over his lighter. "Let's see what you got then and when it goes off, run" says Alex. I inhale largely, and begin the let the flame rise above the lighter; I bring the ball closer. Alex, then pulls out his phone and plays a song. Now I am spinning the ball into all directions so that every part of the ball gets burnt. It takes a bit of time and the boys about are getting bored. "Come on then" Alex says impatiently. Suddenly, boom! And ball catches fire, before it burns my fingertips, I chuck it onto the floor, stamp on it and notice smoke arise. "Wow! Run!" Announces a lad, we all run in different ways and peek back to see the amount of grey smoke furiously rising. I witness how everybody's head turns into the direction of smoke.

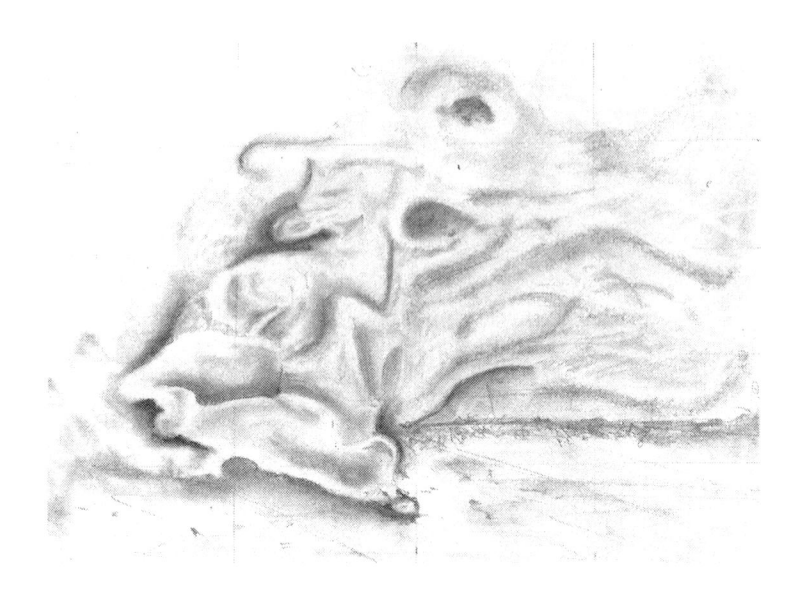

In a matter of seconds, the smoke is the main attraction which draws everyone's attention. Two PE teachers at once run onto the field clearing the students around the smoke away. Steadily the smoke is fading away. My heart is pumping rapidly and I am sweating uncontrollably. I begin to take my jumper off and shove it into my bag. Teachers are observing the area of where I let the smoke off. Students are staring and talking about what just happened. Alex runs towards me. "Give me a snout man" I say. Sam claps me on my back and smilingly states "that was awesome brother, I think you're off the hook." He then handshakes me and hands me a snout. I sit down in the corner of the field and continuously puff onto the cigarette. "Slow down man, you'll choke" speaks Sam.

"That was nuts man! I'm sweating like crazy" I reply.

"Ha-ha, I can see that man, give me a few drags."

I hand the snout over to him; he inhales and exhales the smoke a few times.

FREEZE! I have caused a lot of trouble with Year 7 on its own. In Moore's, if you get into trouble in class, they put something called 'trouble points' on your profile system. In year 7 alone, I got 260 points! That is outrageous! I'll explain and tell you a few.

Some of the troubles/mistakes I have committed which were major but funny, by the way, the teachers have put this up on my profile system and is in their own words.

1. Spanish Teacher: Isaac was being disruptive in class so I asked him to wait outside. When I was trying to talk to him, he said 'get lost, I'll do whatever I want to do'. I then tried to put him in the class next door however then again he told me to get lost and this time he walked off. (5 trouble points)
2. ICT Teacher: Two boys were fighting during class, whilst I tried to get help and stop it, Isaac decided to run towards the fight and abuse one of the boys. Detention needs to be set. (7 trouble points)
3. Wood Tech Teacher: Isaac was incredibly dangerous during the class practical. He first got saw dust and chucked it on his peers which caused them to scream and shout and led to further interruption. Then he got a Metal Filer and threatened his peers that he'd rip their guts out. (8 trouble points)
4. Bypassing Teacher: Isaac ran past me Period 4 and was punching another student—I chased after him, I asked him to stop and he was

verbally aggressive to me, I asked who are you talking to, he said 'you' in a very destructive manner. (5 trouble points)

FREEZE! *Every other incident was similar to the ones I've told you now. This was definitely not the intention I had expected. Simply, I joined the wrong crowd of friends, which led to one thing to another. People do not realise how drastically a person can change. It wasn't even a couple of months till I got caught up in the 'hood life' and I was only in year 7. Every day, was a new day. I walked to school with the Mayhem boys, had regular 'snouts' and do the same old in school; cause havoc. I will explain one other incident that happened in year 7 then I will move onto Year 8 as I have lots to convey. Back to the story . . .*

CHAPTER 7

Fire! Fire!

"So another big plan of ours, let's set the toilets on fire!" Exclaims Alex; our faces show that we are not really sure. "It can lead to bigger things if the fire gets too hard to handle plus the teachers will investigate deeply. We need to be smart about this and need to take a lot of time planning it" speaks one of the boys.

This is quite a big thing to do. If anyone of us gets caught, we can get kicked out. Shall I just drop out on this one? This mission seems is too hard for me and my brain to handle, so I speak out "Alex, sorry man but this seems too risky for me to be part of it."

He seems shocked. "What are you talking about? You are one of the best members we've got in this group. You're sneaky and we have you as an advantage; you're only in year 7 and the teachers will think you wouldn't do such a thing if you got caught." I am confused but feel quite 'big' the way Alex is describing me. You know what? Who cares? I am going to do every flipping mission I have to do.

"I have no clue why I just said that, forget it I'm in and always will be" I announce.

"That's the spirit" says Alex. The rest of Mayhem Crew gives strange looks.

Honestly, I could not give a monkey's no more. I have done so many horrible things; what is the point of stopping? I'm a part of this Crew and always will be, no matter what. We are family and we'll always stick together. Alex states an influential speech that makes the rest of the Crew agree to this daring task. "Do each and one of you know why you are here? Do you know how you got here? Let me tell you. I spotted something 'special' in each individual standing amongst you."

Everyone looks around to one another, feeling praised. Alex continues.

"I thought that if I put a little group together with you people as a part of it, we would be untouchable. Instead of the teachers ruling the school, we'll be the Heads. You got to remember, we always stick together; we never give up. These missions that I set, I'm not dumping it all on you; I do them too. As I told you we're in this together. We need to fight these fears and always strive forward. Missions allow us to see how each and one of us can cope. It builds our confidence, it doesn't lower it. Now tell me, are you in or out? As I told you, we're a family."

My surroundings seem to brighten up; motivation coursed through us. I sense my body tingling with excitement, hyper and jumpy however not just me, the rest of the members too. Alex noticed it too so without asking, he put his hands in the middle; members start to realise and they too put their hands in the middle, on top of Alex's and so forth. I then put my hands on top; gradually everyone's' hands, is in the middle. I notice something, our Crew is multicultural. You can spot it by the different colour of hands, piled up, Diversity which seems fair.

"In 3, 2, 1, shout out, 'Mayhem Crew Will Always Rule!... 3...2...1...!"

All at once, we repeat "Mayhem Crew Will Always Rule!" and raise our hands up above. A loud cheer erupts. We did Alex proud; he is funny, motivating, determined and overall a good leader. To me, he was like an older brother.

After we all calm down, we go to the back of the field. Today, there are many numbers with us. I did not realise till today, how many members there were. Alex pulls out a deck and another two boys do also. They take a snout out and pass it around. There are three cigarette decks to choose from. What is the difference between them? One of the decks comes to me; it reads 'Benson & Hedges Duals'. I take one out. I perceive a blue-like button on the filter. "What's this?" I ask.

"Press the button tightly, it changes the cigarette taste to a mint flavour, it's quite nice" says Carlton.

Impressive; I hold the button and hear a click.

"You've popped it. Now light it up and taste the flavour" says Carlton.

He passes me a lighter and I light it up. I inhale... This actually tastes so nice! I experience the menthol, going down my throat.

"Like it?" asks Carlton.

"Love it!" I respond.

Whilst smoking this mint-flavoured snout, I witness something else. Everyone smokes here! Not just the boys however a few girls are with us too.

In the Crew, there are a couple of girls as members however they do not do the missions we boys do. I remark them as side-girls (followers and basically, we boys use them), they get what the members need e.g. snouts, weed, money etc... That's how the Ghetto Girls are in this school. I should not say this but I also refer them as 'slag's', if you get what I mean. They seem quite desperate. Anyways . . .

Half way through lunch, we are still sitting at the back of the field, gradually a few heads disappear because they went to get some 'munch'. "We will set the fire tomorrow. We will burn the maths block toilets. I haven't decided who will burn the first part but I will tell you how to do it. It's simple, grab the tissue roles from each cubicle, and place them in the middle of the toilets. Scatter them around loosely. Next thing is, light them up. Before you know it, the toilet's going to go up into flames. Lastly, check what direction the camera is facing and when it rotates away, you leg it."

Now that Alex has explained it, it seems like an easy 'assignment' to achieve. The members ask a few questions. I am thinking of volunteering to do the actual action of setting the fire. "Alex, I'll set the fire" I say. He looks amused.

"Okay . . . are you sure yeah?" he asks. I have another quick think and proclaim "Yeah, no problem. I'm up for this!"

Another mission I set myself for. I don't really mind doing it because hey, look on the positive side; I get twice the much of recognition. I believe I am thinking a bit too in the future here; however after Alex leaves high school, I hope to become the new leader of the Mayhem Crew and replace his current position.

That is one thing you have learnt about me, I dream big and expect to achieve despite the other factors.

(The next morning) Today is the day. I am acknowledging mixed emotions. Am I excited, brave or scared? I cannot figure it out just yet. I get ready for school, do the regular procedure. I quickly grab a snack bar,

tell mum that I am leaving and exit the house. I meet the Mayhem boys at the hill. "I heard you asked Alex that you want to set the toilets on fire?" asks one of the Mayhem boys.

"Yeah man, I did" I reply.

"It takes a lot of balls to do that you know, I wouldn't be able to do that . . ." he counters.

"Sometimes you just got to take a risk" I say.

He lightens up as well as the other lad with us. Afterwards, we have a snout and stop by at the shops. I have loose change on me so I go buy a drink. The nerves are taking over slowly every time we take a step closer to school. I try to block them out.

FREEZE! I still cannot believe how I committed this action even till today. What was I doing, I had no clue. I will skip to the Fire scene.

We all have a cigarette and smoke whilst Alex explains. "So this is the plan. George you're looking out for any teachers OUTSIDE the toilet and Carlton, you're looking out on the STAIRS for teachers as well. Isaac, you will collect all the toilet rolls and then light then up in a bundle. After you do that, George has to signal when to run and you only run when the camera isn't facing you; if you get caught then we're busted. Okay, Carlton you will set the fire alarm off and I will race to each nearby classroom and inform the teachers." We listen carefully and nod our heads. "Yep, we can do this, seems easy" says Carlton confidently.

"Never say a mission is easy, you may jinx it and if you flop and get caught, you're going to look like an idiot. Remember to focus at all times. Isaac, do this smoothly and there's no rush" responds Alex.

"Hold on, what is plan B if teachers come or ask us why we aren't in class?" asks George. Us lot agree nodding.

Alex responds, "I didn't come to that part yet but now I will; plan B is distraction. At this point, I will also be looking out for on-lookers behind the lockers. I'll go up to the teacher and make conversation; I then will say 'man-on' casually and after, George will run in the toilets and tell Isaac to stop. I will try my best to drift the teacher to another direction. If you see us out of sight, you make a run for it and grab Carlton while running. Plan B is a bit err . . . rusty but Improvise! We got this man, we're pro's." It is break-time and the bell is about to go in a few minutes. I spray myself in deodorant, chuck a gum in my mouth and walk towards class.

English is boring. The teacher, all she does is tells us to get our books out and read for the whole hour. I do not like her. Currently, I am reading 'the curious incident of the dog in the night-time' by Mark Haddon. The book is incredible even though I hate reading.

So that is what we did throughout the lesson, read. Finally, the bell rings and we pack away. Recently, I have not been 'friends' with anyone in our year. I only talk to a few but they were in my primary school, that's why. Whilst thinking about this, coincidently a boy from our year comes up to me. I do recognise him because he is in a few of my lessons; Maths, History and PE.

"Yo, you're the kid who had the fight init. I rate you man, by the way you're part of the Crew too right?" says the boy. How did he find out about the 'crew'? I ask him.

"Crew? Who told you?" I reply.

"Bruv, my brother used to be the leader of the Mayhem Gang but he left school now. I know who the members are and I see you hang about with them." He responds. I am quite in shock.

"How comes you're not part of it?" I enquire.

"Don't know, thought I was too young and didn't think anyone else in our year would join them but now because you are, I probably will" he responds.

"Ok cool, let's go to Alex and tell him you want to be part of it yeah? And my name's Isaac." I tell him.

"My name's Rezwan and will they make me do anything; like to join the 'crew'?" enquires Rezwan.

"No they won't make you do nothing, don't worry." I reply.

We walk and carry on talking about what primary school we came from and I ask him what missions his brother pulled off.

He laughs and says "one time, my brother's mates and him were rushing someone. He grabbed a bottle and bottled the guy on his head. Apparently, the guy had a spasm on the floor and was knockout. It was peak but quite funny."

Wow, that is a bit extreme. We were outside and the weather is looking on point. Whilst we walk on the field, I look for the crew however find none of them. I spiral round trying to examine their present location. I do it a few more times and on the fifth, I spot Carlton's green jacket. Why on earth are they in the far right of the field, dumping in a corner?

"There they are" I say.

Rezwan trails behind. "You're Bengali right?" I ask.

"Yeah, I am" he replies. He dips his hands into his pockets and kicks the grass. "By the way, do you smoke?" I enquire.

"A bit man, but don't tell no-one" responds Rezwan. While we are still making our way to the Crew, Rezwan says "I want to bunk one time." I smile and tell him that I have already done it before. He looks shocked and asks me how it felt doing it for the first time. I explain to him that the adrenaline rushes and nerves combined together make you even more excited. He looks stimulated.

"When you going to do it next because I want to come with you" he asks.

"Shouldn't be a problem . . ." I reply.

We finally reach the whereabouts of the Crew and I see Alex.

"Come over here!" he mumbles.

We walk faster. Alex gives Rezwan a cheesy grin.

"So you finally decide to follow your brother's footsteps. You want to join?" utters Alex.

Oh, so they already know each other and he just asked if he wanted to join. I guess I do not need to introduce them to each other and request Alex if Rezwan can join. That made it simpler.

We both handshake each person and Rezwan says "yeah that's why Isaac bought me to you."

"My two younger's, the Crew gets better and better; you're in." Alex speaks proudly. After a while, I ask Alex why they are here and not at the back.

"Because one of our Muppets was smoking, standing up and the teacher clocked on, now the idiot is in seclusion" he explains.

"So is this area safe? I question.

"As long as you ain't a muppet" Alex winks.

He hands me a cigarette, he offers Rezwan one too but he tells him that he will share with me.

Sharing a cigarette is called two's or three's. Rezwan calls two's which means I give him the cigarette half way.

Gradually, Alex and the rest slowly drift away till it is left with Rezwan and me alone. Us two talk more and more about different things and we did not realise we are talking so much till the bell rings for end of lunch. Before he walks off to registration, I say "This is it; I got to set the toilets on fire" he laughs and I continue to talk "get ready to line up for the fire alarm and don't make it obvious to the others." I handshake him and stroll off.

It feels good to have another 'friend' after Philip left. I hope Rezwan and me can be best friends too because he seems cool, I suppose. My mind moves away to thinking of the mission. I'm meant to leave now so I tell the Form Tutor that I'm going to the toilet (which indeed I am). I stride quickly to the maths block toilets. A few teachers walk pass however I dare not to give eye contact due to the reason being, I suspect them to see my nerves by looking me in the eyes, quite strange right? I step up the stairs and am happy to see Carlton, already in position. "Ready little man?" he asks. I give him a handshake and reply

"Think so . . . ." Vigilantly, I look up toward the ceiling, where the camera is, and luckily it is facing in my opposite direction. I open the double doors widely and take a couple more steps, take a right and then enter the toilets. I see George looking into the mirror. He turns around immediately after seeing my reflection. Instantly, he hands me a lighter, says good luck and pats me on my shoulder; he seems more nervous than me! I did not even have the chance to ask him where Alex is, however he may be on patrol, looking out too. I see George also carefully hearing out for any footsteps that are close by approaching his direction. "Right, lets get started" I mutter to myself. From cubicle to cubicle, I reach and drag out each toilet roll, stuffing them close up to my chest. There are 6 cubicles in here so I will scatter the toilet paper, messily. I am in such a hurry that the nerves are starting to drift. Finally, after gathering all the paper, I pull out the one and only . . . lighter; the item that will set off the alarms and cause 'Mayhem'. I flick the metal part of the lighter; only sparks appear no flame. I shake it at once and try again. This time it works and I begin to lower the lighter, I close my left eye, peeking through the right and set the first part of the roll on fire.

Only a few seconds went by and the fire is increasing. I try to make use of every roll and bundle it over the flame. This is scary! I am absolutely terrified! I think George smelt the smoke and he turns around. His eyes gawk towards the fire like an owl. He signals me to come out and I do so. After I get out, he pulls me back, checks where the camera is facing and when it is clear, we leg it. As soon as we run out, we open the door and George tells Carlton to smash the fire alarm button. We are on the last bunch of staircases when suddenly the ear-splitting alarm goes off. Afterwards, when Carlton catches up, we see Alex running to each Form class notifying the teacher. These pupils are crazy! Especially our year! "Fire! Fire!" Yells the immature students; "we're gonna die!!" they continue. All three of us run out onto the playground. Already, Form classes are out onto the other side of the ground and are getting in register order. Together, we run and try to find our individual forms. George spots his and sprints to them. After that, Carlton finds his and he runs to his class. After a little bit of a wonder, I see my class coming out from the Science doors. "Isaac! Isaac!" Screams the form tutor "We're here, join the line!"

Terrified does not even describe how I am feeling right now. I feel as if I am about to piss my pants. We line up on the tennis court in alphabetical order, depending on your surname. I hear student names being called out from all directions. I daze off, worrying about the consequences of what will happen if we get caught.

"Isaac . . . Isaac!" Bellows the teacher, "stop daydreaming and listen!"

I shake my head and reply "oh . . . oh, sorry miss!"

She then continues. I also resume and think again about the consequences.

People start to moan and groan because they are tired of standing up. "Only a few more minutes!" announces a teacher. In the distance, I hear the sound of a Fire Truck siren. Rapidly, students turn their head towards the oncoming vehicle. I hear an older kid with a Yorkshire accent, saying "Oh ma god, this isn't a fake! It's real it is. Ma blooming god, imagine if somebody was in there right naw, burning alive!"

I am actually trying to picture in my head if someone is in fact in there. Many questions jump into my brain. What if someone dies because of me? Will I be classed as a murderer? Are the police getting involved? What if they find any evidence?! The nerves have finally taken over my body. I did not even realise that I am sweating like a pig. Straight away, I grab my deodorant and squirt it out. "Stop that! It's disgusting" moans a girl behind me. I give her a straight face look and put the spray back into my bag.

FREEZE! For this incredible stupid action of mine, I luckily didn't get caught. In fact no-one got caught. That was the end of it. Year 7 was an absolute rollercoaster and it was time for me to make a change (in Year 8) however nothing really improved even though I tried to make progress. Roll on Year 8!

CHAPTER 8

Fresh Start

The summer holidays are now over and it is time to get ready for school. Yawning, I drag myself out of bed; however it seems as if the bed keeps pulling me back in. It is quite hard, waking up at 7:15am after being so used to sleeping in and waking up late.

At last, I manage to drag myself out and sleepwalk to the bathroom. I throw ice-cold water at my face in a vain attempt to wake my body up; luckily it worked. To myself, I think today will be the start of a new day, the positive way. I stare long and hard at my reflection. I look deep into my eyes. This is quite scary because when I look into my eyes for a bit too long, it seems as if my face does not belong to me, it is a strangers characteristics. I continue with my usual routine of getting ready for school however I apply additional 'things to do' because it is the first day of Year 8 (I prefer not to say what they are).

"Bye Mum!" I announce.

"Have a good day honey!" She responds.

I close the door behind me and close my eyes, inhale and begin to make the first few steps. I smile as I see a few familiar faces that go to our school. I like school, there is new drama everyday e.g. Fights! Moore's Academy News Feed. I remember this one time in year 7 when I witnessed a girl fight. Oh my days! First of all, the girl from our school chased another girl from elsewhere. After she caught up with her, they start pulling one another's hair. Mainly our school kids were there to watch it and then out of the blue, girls start jumping in. Our school girls were literally kicking the crap into this one girl. Shockingly, the girl that was on the floor, her mother came out. She just violated these school girls. Then even more girls joined the fight and abused both the mother and daughter. It was absolutely horrendous! The next day, one of the girls that got involved; her arm had a gigantic plaster on it. When I asked her what happened, she told me that when she had the mother in a headlock, the mother must've been quite hungry and chewed onto her arm like a dog. Nasty!

Once I get up to the hill, I see no sign of the Mayhem Boys. I decide to wait for a bit. Did they forget about me? Fortunately, after a bit of time, the two boys appear in front of me together, breathlessly "so . . . rry . . . we . . . we . . . woke up . . . late."

"Ha-ha, don't worry, I thought you two left without me" I reply.

They both lean up against a brick wall for a few seconds and then we continue to walk. "Give me a snout man" asks one of the Mayhem boys.

"I haven't got none, I thought you did" responds the other.

I jump in and say "I haven't got none either"

"Great, no snouts till we reach the shops!" says the boy that is craving for a cigarette. I also did feel the urge to have a snout as I am used to having one at this time. We would have jogged however none of us are in the mood.

As soon as we got to the shops, one of the boys, Callum goes in to the shop to purchase a deck. The other one follows to buy a drink because he seems dehydrated. I wonder outside the shops and observe Callum at the counter. I notice the shopkeeper giving the deck and Callum giving a fiver in return. Seriously, what if I was an undercover police; I just witnessed a shopkeeper serving cigarettes to an underage youth. But at least we do get served right?

Without delay, one pulls out a lighter and Callum unwraps the deck. Callum takes one out passes one to me and I hand one over to the other Mayhem boy. Peaceful, we smoke with no disruption plus we have 20 minutes to get to school. Callum lights up another cigarette, I reject the second one. "You can two's with me" says the other Mayhem boy. Smoking one after another is called 'chain-smoking'. Interesting how we come up with these really.

We maintain our journey to school. Once we get in, I notice everyone handshaking and hugging each other. "It was only the summer holidays and look how big you've grown!" says a student passing by. Oh please, be quiet. Most people are overreacting. I make my usual way to the canteen and handshake the lads. "How was your summer holiday? Questions a lad in my year; "Fine." I answer.

School goes the usual way, the teachers' greets us back and we resume class work. This year, I hope to improve; I will put my head down in every subject and cause fewer nuisances. Also, I will show more respect to the teachers and listen to most of their instructions. This will definitely be a new me, I hope.

FREEZE! All I did was rely on hope. Actually, I did improve in lessons and was putting my head down. However due to last year's trouble, the teachers obviously still had a negative insight of me. I was in fact quite quieter in lessons. Before I used to be a big-mouth; I think it was a bit of a shock to everyone that I wasn't speaking, or in the teachers' case, shouting much. To conclude, I did something in Moore's East Academy drove me to getting kicked out. I shall explain from the start to end which led me to get excluded.

CHAPTER 9

Trails and Clues

Recently, I took on boxing. The coach said I had a natural talent in the sport and that I could be allocated in having a skill bout with another opponent in a few months. From then on, I focused on boxing at all times. After school today, I have training.

It's lunch time and Alex informs all of our members to meet up at the new location on the field. We rarely have urgent gatherings so this must be important indeed. Right away, I walk towards the field. I see several of other members making their way too and I walk with them also. "I wonder what this is about . . ." states a girl which is part of the crew. As soon as we spot Alex, we walk in a faster pace. It is as if he is our God and we obey him. To be honest he is kind of God's gift; he's excellent at everything really.

Alex begins to speak, "It's good that most of us came today. The reason I made all of you come is because I think we need a break. We need to relax with the 'missions' due to not giving out clues to the teachers. Otherwise, they will figure out that it was us creating all the problems in school. The fire; the teachers are still on the case. Luckily, they haven't identified any names but they found a few traces such as finger prints. So, Carlton, when you hit the fire alarm button, were you wearing gloves?"

Everyone stares at Carlton. "Erm . . . I don't think so?"

A slight frustration moan is conveyed by a couple of members.

"The reason I asked you was because they wanted to know who set off the alarm to see who the closet was when the fire was increasing. At the moment, they think it was a teacher that set it off but if they do examine the finger print further, there maybe trouble. It may expose us all but let's just hope nothing happens." Replies Alex.

There is an awkward silence. I observe the fear on peoples face, especially mine. I am thinking about the consequences that may occur if the police and school figure out is was me that actually set the fire. I would probably be put into prison and given a never-ending sentence! That thought made my body shiver. After Alex has finished talking, we slowly start to disappear. I can hear members criticising Carlton. "What the hell is wrong with you man?!" "Wear gloves next time!" "If you get clocked, you better not snitch on us!"

At once Carlton responds "Shut up, do you know how much pressure I was in? Half of you weren't even there so you can't talk." Everybody silences.

I line up to get something to eat.

I purchase a tuna and sweet-corn baguette before I make my way to the back of the cafeteria hall. "Sit next to us" says Rezwan.

"Its cool man, I'll sit by myself." Rezwan gathers his belongings and comes to my lonely table to join me.

"What's wrong?" he asks.

"Apparently, there's a chance for us getting caught. Carlton wasn't wearing gloves when he smashed the button and now forensics got involved! What if I also get caught man? I'll be in big trouble!" I react.

Rezwan responds "Oh no, but don't think about it brother, block it out and think about the present. There's no point stressing over it right now. My mum always told me, if you stress over something that might happen; it will happen." My eyes lit up and immediately I attempt not to think about it.

"Give me a bit" asks Rezwan. I break the baguette into half and give him the bigger piece. "Thanks man" praises Rezwan; "now, let's finish eating and go play a bit of football."

He's a nice friend; at least he cares, right? After a few minutes we head towards the field, not to smoke, not to muck about, but to play football; like the previous days, back in primary school.

"Haven't seen you play in a while" conveys Marcus (one of my mates back in the days)

He separates Rezwan and me into different sides. I'm beginning to play football again; thanks to Rezwan. Already, I have set up two goals and scored one my-self. The weather is banging! However it is a bit too hot. As sweat drips from my forehead, I begin to take off my jumper and pop on my trainers. The ball reaches to my feet and I dribble with the ball. I get pass two players so far and people in my team call out my name for the ball however I reject their offer. As I continue to dribble, I notice that I am getting closer and closer to the goal and not going in different angles. I lift my leg back, wait for the clear chance to take the shot, I shoot . . . I score! It's absolutely unbelievable, I dribble past their whole team and manage to score which puts our team in the lead. Our players begin to cheer and next thing you know is, they are on top of me, a dog-pile. We won the game by one goal, thanks to me. "Well played Isaac, from now on we'll play more often" congratulates Rezwan as well as a few other players. I believe this is the first step towards 'improving' in school as I did not get up to any mischief today. I feel proud of myself. Later on during the day, after school; I prepare for boxing.

I wrap my boxing straps onto my hands, put on my boxing shorts plus the vest and fill up my water bottle. Our gym is not too far away from where our house is located, it is only 7 minutes away by walking however our coach tells us to jog to the gym and that only takes me 4 minutes. I have got to admit, my stamina is actually really good. In year 7, I was chosen to run for the school cross county team against all-schools. There is ten minutes left but as I am an impatient being, I leave the house. I stuff earphones in and make my journey to the gym, jogging. In addition whilst I jog, I also shadow box the thin air. It's quite weird punching air when by-passers walk or drive pass although, in my opinion they look at you with a bit of respect. Sometimes I notice the fear in their eyes which shows that they would not want to mess with you. I'm huffing and puffing however I'm nearly there. I am listening to 'Sneakbo—Real Talk.' Yup, my type of music is Grime mostly.

I finally reach the road of the gym and see our coach jogging too. I sprint up towards him and greet him. He does not respond back so I assume that he is feeling exhausted as he has a longer journey of getting here. We both slow down and walk into the entrance. He then handshakes me and pats me on my back. "Go inside the hall and tell the other boys to help set up" orders the coach. We call the coach 'COMMANDO', I really did not know why however that is what he tells us to call him. "Commando says to set up!" I announce; it is a Wednesday today and 9 of our boxers turn up.

Wednesday's are only for boxers with more potential, such as: having bouts, and to have bouts you have to be a good boxer. Together as a team, we put up the 2 boxing bags, 10 skipping ropes, the timer, and 6 pairs of boxing gloves alongside the rest of the gear. As soon as Commando enters, I volunteer to lead the warm up. We start off with 8 laps around the hall even if you have jogged to the gym. During the laps we do high knees, heel flicks and side to side types. I can spot out the people that are already drained out. One of the lads, Zayn; his boxing style is top. He has incredible speed and the way he moves around the ring is interesting to watch however his stamina is nil. It really lets him down. Apparently, he is a heavy smoker and other boxers say heavy does not even describe the amount he smokes. I don't care if I am smoker, my stamina is still living but I know that if I do stop, it will improve, oh well. After we done our laps, I lead the stretches; "starting from your head guys, a circular motion but don't go too quickly" I say to the boys. I witness the coach looking at me, he is smiling. After the stretches, we skip for 3 rounds, 1 minute and 30 seconds and 30 second break. We do different types of skipping also, crossovers, double jumps, high knees and run skips. Moving on from that, we do shadow boxing. Commando opens the mirror cabinet which then allows us to see our reflection, "shadow box boxers!" Orders Commando

This allows us to see our movements and the motions of our punches. Speed is a key. 30 minutes into the session, another coach enters. Immediately the coach pulls out the pads and announces "line up for pad work!" Three boxers rush over.

"Isaac and Zayn, get your gum-shields in and head guards on." Says Commando, time for a bit of sparring, the coaches say that I have got immense power in my punches and that I need to improve on my speed. My footwork is standard for an amateur boxer and my hands are always up defensively. I really like boxing because my type of sport is always to get in physical contact. When I spar, I imagine ripping the opponent's guts out. I never take it easy, spar me or don't however, I will never step down.

Commando sets the timer, 1 minute and 30 seconds for 3 rounds. I put on the blue head guard and one of the boxers helps me put on the blue Adidas gloves. I position myself in my corner. My stronger hand is my left one therefore I should be boxing with a southpaw stance however I find it more comfortable boxing with an orthodox stance with my left hand in front. This is an advantage as my jabs will be more powerful, steering my opponent away from me. Before the sparring is about to take action, Commando gives me a bit of advice, "keep your head up, and don't turn your head when your opponent is punching you. Defensive wise, you're good so remember to keep your gloves up. Zayn has got speedy punches but remember to give the double jabs and hook to the ribs." All the boxers gather around the ring; "round 1, box!" Announces Commando; we begin. Zayn starts to jump around like a kangaroo. I wait for him to throw the first punch, so that I can counter attack. He leans in for a jab and I hit it out with my glove and release a hook to his body, it skims him. Without thinking, I attack with the 2 jabs and 1 hook to the body movement. This made Zayn wobble which is a good sign. As I see him unstable, I begin my moves; rapidly I punch him, starting with the face, down to the body. "Keep your guard and head up Zayn!" shouts Commando.

I shuffle backwards, jumping back and forth. From his eyes, I can tell that he is angry. Without prior notice, Zayn goes in with venomous punches. 3 connect to my nose, and 1 connects with my chest. Now, I'm pissed! I discharge many jabs and he does the same. "Stop street fighting!" Screws Commando; the timer goes off; letting us know that round 1 is officially over. The coach that helps us out goes to Zayn to advise him. Commando comes to me. "Excellent boxing lad, but remember not to throw wild punches! I know Zayn does, but you keep your guard up and get closer to him so it is harder for him to throw punches." He pours water into my mouth. I kind of dribble; "Get back into your positions" orders Commando. He takes the centre of the ring and shouts "Round 2, box!" I scuffle forward, jabbing so that my opponent retreats. He isn't releasing his fists so I believe he may be going for the counter attack shots. After discovering that I am correct, I too play mind games. I dummy punches and often give him the hooks to the body. I am planning to give him an uppercut. My mind makes up the decision, and I go for the shot. He blocks the uppercut and throws a punch, directly to my nose which causes me to shuffle back, "nice clean shot" says the helping-out coach. That shot makes me extra alert for any other incoming shots. Both of us circulate around the ring, waiting for one of us to punch. I notice that his face is covered however not his ribs therefore I go for the shot. Bang! A clear connected hook that leaves Zayn unstable on his feet. Instantly, he lifts up his hands, signalling to stop. He spits out his gum shield and hold onto his left side rib. He is winded. Commando rushes over. "Why did you keep your body open?!" complains Commando.

"Give me . . . a sec" says Zayn, trying to catch his breath. I stand there, neutrally. "Nice shot Isaac" praises a boxer. The timer then beeps, informing us that round 2 is over. He crouches and walks to his corner. "Breath in and out" recommends coach.

"Superb shot! Stay alert all the time. There's only one round left, show me that you're ready for your skill bout in 3 weeks" speaks Commando. I suddenly become more energetic and a bit more aggressive. Dog-like, I chew onto my gum shield, tensing my teeth together. "Seconds out, last round" initiates Commando. The final beep rings. We both again, flow in a circle. Eye to eye, we watch our moves. None of us dare to jab just yet. Our surroundings monitor every movement. I start off with 2 jabs and a hook however he rejects all the shots and startlingly, does not punch back. I am trying to figure out what kind of mind game he is trying to play now. Expect the unexpected is what I am trying to play, so leading on from that, I jab rapidly. His elbows are tucked in neatly which protects his ribs and face. When I figure out that there is no point, I repel away. I can see his eyes blazing however he does not appear to hit me back. With the corner of Zayn's eye, I see him looking at the timer, showing there is only 45 seconds left. His shoulders seem more relaxed and I definitely expect him to hit back. Eventually I am right and he releases with two fearsome jabs to my nose.

I stumble backwards and ultimately fall to the ground. An awkward silence takes place. I get back onto my feet, shake my head and wipe my gloves onto my vest. "You alright?" asks Commando.

"Yeah . . . Yeah" I respond inattentively. I reposition into my stance; he is really going to get a piece of me now. However before I begin to punch witlessly, I remember that Commando told me to prevent doing that.

There is only 20 seconds left and neither of us goes in for the strike. So he's playing games, then I shall too. We continue to circulate around. "10 seconds!" shouts Commando desperately. Still Zayn doesn't hit me so I won't either, although surprisingly, I release a two jab and a two hook combination that leaves him flattened on the ground followed by the sound of the finishing round set off by the timer. I hear Commando chuckle quietly. I stand close by to Zayn and help him up. We both take our gloves off and we handshake and give a manly hug to one another. "Nice one" honours Zayn.

"That was good . . ." I respond.

Commando begins to announce, "Fantastic boxing, the pair of you; that's how to box and the lads represented that really well. They've definitely got a bout coming up sooner or later, and if the rest of you want one too, show me that you're ready! Dave and Cameron, get your gum shields on. You've seen a good example of how boxers box properly so show me what you've learnt. Impress me, I dare you."

Coach pats me on my back and Commando lightly slaps the back of my head in a friendly way.

With saliva slipping off my gum shield, I quickly wash it in the toilets and place it back in its usual case. "That ending KO'd me man." Complains Zayn, I smirk back and say "I think you've placed my nose in a crooked direction Bruv." Then again we handshake and at the same time I can hear the thumps landing, it is coming from the ring. Cameron is getting demolished! That's the end of him, I guess.

__FREEZE!__ So I took on boxing, a distraction from all the crap I was doing which is what I'd call progress. I enjoyed it very much and at the time, was looking forward to the fight they were trying to allocate me in. I did notice some change physically, I was getting fitter and losing a lot of weight plus my concentration was improving in school. Carrying on . . .

"Where do you think you lot are going?" Commando challenges. "We're going jogging and then you can go home." We slightly moan as we are already out of energy however we have to listen to the rules. Throughout the last couple of sessions, I was getting extra training time and I currently am now too. I am having a fight on the 23rd November and progressing effectively. After sessions, I stay back an extra ½ an hour to progress on movement and pad-work. I portray myself as Mike Tyson: box with power, avoid shots and react with counter ones instead. I hope to take this sport further in life. Muhammad Ali's quote is always in my head, 'float like a butterfly, sting like a bee'.

When I eventually get to the house, my mum asks me how boxing went. "It was incredible! I'm having a fight soon!"

I witness that smile on her face despite the fact she does not like me boxing, obviously because a mother doesn't want to see her son get punches thrown at him. I begin to shadow box in the living room, trying to catch my mother's attention to see her sons boxing skills. Hyperactively, I run upstairs and grab my items and clothes that I will need. After the shower, I will eat and sleep, normal routine.

Next day, I wake up for school; do the usual. Today, I don't know why but my mum orders me to walk with my sister. "Why?" I ask confusingly.

"Because you go to the same school and don't walk together. Brothers should protect their sisters so do as you're told" clarifies mother.

Without further ado, I wait for my sister to apply the crap on her face (make-up). It is kind of awkward walking school with your sister. As soon we set off, I walk ahead of her. "Walk alone" I taunt.

"Mum said to walk together so come back here" she replies.

"Oh be quiet, you seriously want to walk with your brother?" I counter.

She explodes with a wide mouth full of laughter. "Mothers orders, wasteman" she mocks.

I get a little angry and continue to make my own journey to school. When my sister is out of sight, I turn right into another alleyway. This way will also lead me to my usual route; where the Mayhem boys are too. I rush towards the end of the alleyway. Just about, I can see the light at the end. Closer and closer I get, I hear familiar voices. "Let's just go, he's probably ill or something."

"Okay . . ." agrees the other voice. It got me wondering and soon after, I knew it is the Mayhem Boys. Gasping for breath, I exit the tunnel and find myself directly in front of them. By the looks on their faces, they seem awfully confused. One after another, I look up at them.

"What the . . .?" states one of the lads.

I begin to giggle as their faces look incredibly puzzled. "Running away from the sister you see" I convey as I finally catch some oxygen. A slight laughter goes around and we then the three if us resume. "Chuck us a lighter" I ask. I get passed a lighter and smoothly, begin to light the snout that I carried in my pocket. "You usually don't carry any on you, where'd you get that one from?" raises ones the boys; I grin and reply.

"Kind of a funny story, Dad was asleep, I was in his room. My eye caught the loose deck in his pocket. I was scared at first but was kind of craving. Before you knew it, I slipped a single out." I observe the 'cool/easy' look on the two boys.

"Bigger balls I see" says the boy.

"Yeah yeah . . ." I counter.

FREEZE! I was gradually improving in school. However my mind was focused on boxing. That is all I cared about. Before you resume with the book, I will skip to my boxing fight as I have plenty to portray. This was the part which led to get excluded permanently from Moore's East Academy. You may continue . . .

CHAPTER 10

Skill Bout

Sweat trickles down my forehead. Slowly, the nerves rush through my body mixed with a bit of my adrenaline rush. I'm ready . . . I think. Things are getting intense as boxers are getting changed and coaches are doing a bit of pad-work. I have been allocated to the 'red' changing rooms. Red indicates the boxers that are from Luton (therefore I get changed there). I am not aware who my opponent is or where he is from. The most I know about him is, he is 49.2 kg and I am 49 kg dead on. I can win this, I know I can. With motivation surrounding my mind, I get some horrific images in my head. I hope I rip this lad's heart out and crush him to dust. I will break all of his teeth and simply tear this waste of a boxer. Commando comes in and helps me to be prepared. He pulls out the pads from his backpack. I begin to wrap on my boxing straps. I take my time and do this carefully as I want to have comfortable, relaxing hands and no pressure. "You've got this Isaac; he isn't experienced in a ring so you've got your shot. Make our wish come true" advises Commando.

I like him. He's a real nice guy. Fantastic coach also.

Commando assists me with my gloves and I lift my hands and gain my stance. He shouts a number and a combination I should perform. I do as I am told. However, it does get a bit awkward as other boxers from your town watching you and eying up your technique. Strangely, it does motivate me to, you know, show off a little. Everyone stops what they are doing, including me. "Welcome to the Boxwell Amateur boxing show. Thank you for everyone turning up today and I hope our boxers on tonight's show can impress you. Without further ado, I welcome you to opening boxers of the show" announces the host of tonight's boxing.

The door creaks open, "Matthew Brennings, would you like to come this way please" says a guy who has one of them ear pieces, on his right ear; it's one of those spy items, the one you see in the movies. He inhales and exhales before taking his first steps. I presume he is the first boxer, opening the show. A few of the other boxers say good luck, so I do too. The pressure is rising. Startlingly, my hands start to shake and to stop it, I clinch my fists, following with a 360 degrees rotation with my neck. I jump up and down and punch my fists towards the ground. On my left, I notice a couple of fighters looking at the wall. "Isaac Ingham's up next" announces a boxer with red and white stripy shorts.

"That's me" I convey.

"You're up next mate" he speaks. "Good luck"

"Safe" I reply. Commando taps me on my back and pours a little drop of water on top of my head. "You've got this" he encourages.

"I hope so" I respond. In the distance, I can hear many cheers. The bell rings indicating round 1 is over. "Round out!" notifies the ref. I start to shadow box, it helps me focus. Commando is called to go outside. I try to listen what they're saying. "Your boxer is up next" says the person speaking to Commando, "wait outside the double doors and we'll tell you when to come in."

"Thanks" replies Commando. He comes back into the changing rooms. I pick up my water bottle and gum shield, I hand them over to Commando. Before leaving, he gives me last minute advice. "Remember everything I've taught you. Keep your hands up and don't drop them, defence is a key. Also, don't release wild shots and focus on your accuracy. And the main point, give it your best and rip him apart."

I take in everything he says.

Commando and I stand outside the double doors. Surprisingly, the coach that helps us out appears a couple of steps to my right. He begins to speak "Sorry for being late, couldn't find parking. I just made it in time, Isaac, good luck boxer."

Commando makes a conversation with him however my centre of attention is towards the fight, "An excellent fight by the two boxers. A round of applause please" portrays the host. A loud clapping of hands fills up the arena. "The winner by judge's decision is, Bryon Filler!" states the host. Oh no, Matthew didn't win. This loss from one of our town boxers de-motivates me a little. A few seconds later, Matthew opens the door and his head is down. "Well done mate" I tell him. I offer a handshake. Then again the man with the ear-piece comes outside. "Ready?" he says. We begin to walk in the arena. The speaker above me is playing an instrumental. Immediately, I notice that it's called Android porn.

The sound of the beat pumps my blood giving me additional adrenaline. Walking/jumping to the ring, I detect two of my mates from Moore's. One smiles and I do in return. The crowd are pulling their phones out, I'm assuming to record my fight. I see my opponent. Roughly, I witness that he is a little shorter than me and has a bit of a wide upper body. He looks straight into my eyes. Commando stretches the ropes and I crouch to enter the ring. He places my gum shield into my mouth. I bite as hard as possible before having to put on my gloves. "Remember your counter shots" says Commando. "He hasn't got fast punches so control your jabbing. Also, don't look at his gloves, stare into his eyes."

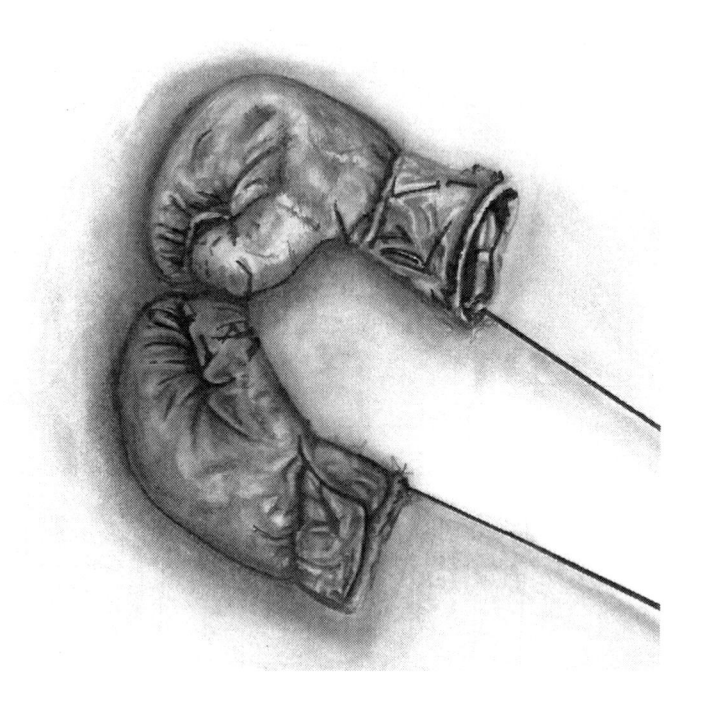

I take in a deep breath and after 3 seconds I breathe out. "Step forward" orders the ref. "You will obey my instructions, when I say break, you break. Keep cool and box; touch gloves." We connect our gloves together before returning back to our corner. The ref comes to me and checks my gloves, groin protector, gum shield and head guard, Commando and coach handshake the ref. After the ref goes to the other boxer to do the same thing, "Focus" says 'coach'. I begin to jump up and down to relax myself. Slowly, I begin to take my stance. The judges take their roles and the ref comes to the centre of the ring. He looks at each of us and then nods. "Box!" Shouts ref. I move into the centre of the ring. Straight away,

I release a double jab. One of the shots connects with the top of his head guard. Numerous shots fly out by the two of us.

The round ends with a positive boxing welcome. In my opinion, I reckon I got more points in the first round, I hit him accurately. Commando takes my gum shield out of my mouth. At once, he inserted a straw in my mouth which is attached to my water bottle. I begin to suck in the refreshing water.

He gives me a quick pep talk. "Keep your eyes focussed. Don't wear yourself out and try to keep hitting him. Instead, move around in the ring and use all of its space. Keep your head up lad; you can take this one on." Carefully, I listen. After a few seconds, the words sink into my head. "Seconds out!" announces ref. I stand up, and gain my stance again. "Relax" mutters Commando. The bells connect and the ref shouts, box! Round 2, let's go! Surprisingly, my opponent dives straight in with venomous punches. I defend my body and my face as if I'm huddling. I cannot see due to the wild shots. I take the risk and release untamed shots back. I am expecting the crowd to see a bunch of youngsters punching as if they're on the streets. In the background, I can hear cheers and awkward shouts. Eventually, I clinch onto my opponent and we let go. Expecting that my opponent will do the same again, I stay active on my toes. I jump about in the ring, causing his jabs to flow and hit the air. My mind tells me to give him that one body shot that would simply leave him 'breathless'. However, I am not that stupid to just hit him, in my mind I plan it out. Accuracy is the key as well as timing. We continue to circulate around the ring without punching. Quickly, I look at the right side of his ribs. Obviously, I have to 'quickly' look so that he doesn't get any hints that, that's where I am going to land my next punch. My opponent releases another combo, however I reject the shots. As soon as I see his ribs open, Bam! I connect directly onto his ribs; he immediately reacts with the shot.

From the way he is stumbling, I know that he is winded. At this point, it is my turn to finish him off.

As my opponent is almost in the corner, I threaten him with vicious jabs so that he gets backed up even more. Now he is trapped in the corner, I automatically hit him non-stop. I don't stop; I just remain jabbing and hooking until the ref came and separated us. As soon as my opponent unclenches me, he falls down onto the ring. I had to go to the corner whilst the ref examines my opponent. The ref begins to count, "1 . . .2 . . .3 . . ."

Finally, my challenger starts to get up. The ref can also tell that he is injured, "you alright? Wipe your gloves onto the vest" instructs the ref. My opponent does so and the ref shouts box.

I know that this is the chance to completely finish him off and, at the back of my mind; I also know that I have definitely won this. Here we go again, and straight away I enable hefty bangs onto his body. Just as I am about to release an uppercut, the bell rings. Round 2 is done and dusted. Luckily for my opponent; he has time to recover and get advice. I walk over to my corner. Commando begins to speak, "that was excellent performance Isaac. Keep it up and now it's your chance to give it your all. All the energy you have left, take it out onto the guy opposite you. You've got the win, keep it up and remember not to give wild punches. Accuracy is the key." As I am sinking in the words again, Coach pours a bit of water down my back. I'm presuming it helps you cool down. I sip in a large amount of water and Commando fans me down, with my towel. This feels so relaxing however my mind is still set on my opponent.

"Seconds out" indicated the ref. Then again, I gain my stance and this time, I'm completely focused. I'm going to steal tonight's show, no matter what. Let me express what I am made of; "final round!" Informs ref, the bells also connect. Strangely, the both of us don't just run in. I'm guessing that he is still determined to win. I step closer and let my jabs flow. He reacts efficiently and circulates. I find no hope in doing this so I give up. I need another plan, quick. Probably, my opponent is thinking to give me that one deadly shot that will leave me on the floor. This thought makes me more defensive. Without thinking straight forwardly, I come up with the most ridiculous plan. I am going to fight like Prince Naseem. Before you know it, I drop my hands and do the moonwalk. My opponent looks lost. The crowd begin to cheer me on, "Isaac! Isaac!" Lord knows how they found out my name.

My opponent starts to get ready. I can observe his hands ready to fly straight into my face. Another stupid move I pull off is, I mock around. I indicate him to hit my jaw as I close my eyes and tap my jaw. He looks furious. Without warning, he begins to hit me. Well, he 'tries'. All the shots he is currently trying to give, they are just wild ones so you cannot assume where they are going to land. My opponent has me in the corner, he can finish me off. I try to doge the crazy shots however I am saved by the bell, knowing that our bout is now over, I put my hands down. As soon as I release them, my challenger gives me a dirty cheap shot onto my temple. "Stop!" shouts the ref. I feel dazed. "Points are deducted, 1 point each judge!" Commando steps into the ring and helps me to sit down in our corner. He speaks, "Don't worry about that cheap shot, you came here to win which you most likely did, I'm sure of it."

I shake my head and Commando takes my gloves and head guard off. I feel a slight breeze. I turn around and see my opponent just staring at me. The ref is talking to him. I did feel a bit frightened as his eyes indicate that he would kill me at any given second. I grin at him to take the piss following a nod to show 'no harm done.' Afterwards, I walk into the centre of the ring, so does my opponent. The ref collects a piece of paper from each judge and examines them. After a couple of minutes, the host announces, "A brilliant fight by our two boxers! A round of applause please", after the clapping, he carries on speaking "there is a black Audi outside, blocking the entrance, the registration plate is AD56 TRE. Please move the car as soon as possible." There is a slight pause before the host continues, "the winner by unanimous decision is, Isaac Ingham!" I jump into the air! The feeling is amazing! I hug my opponent, a manly hug. He accepts the hug. I go over to my opponent's corner and handshake his coaches. Then, I climb out of the ring, over the moon.

I get navigated to the trophy table and I get handed over the 'winners' trophy. I take a picture with my opponent and he tells me his name is Patrick. I then again, handshake followed by a hug him.

I am so happy right now. As I'm in the changing room getting changed into my tracksuit, my two mates from Moore's enter the room, one of them is Rezwan. "You smashed it man!" says the other mate. "That was total violation bro!" Rezwan says.

I accept their praise and thank them. I take my phone out from my gym side bag and begin to type. I go on Blackberry Messenger, (BBM for short) and upload my status, 'I won my fight! Ripped my opponent apart!' After that, I take a picture of my trophy and upload it as my display picture (DM for short). Straight away, 3 of my boys send a congratulations message.

"Yo, I recorded your fight, should I send it?" proclaims Rezwan. I pass him my phone and tell him to Bluetooth it. He agrees and starts the transfer. Commando comes in and see's us three lads hovering around the room. He walks up to me and first thing he does is offer me a handshake and says, "you made me smile boxer, sorry I took so long but another coach was asking for your details"

"Why's that?" I ask.

"One of his boxers is looking for a skill bout and he thinks you're perfect as an opponent." Commando explains. I give a cheesy smile and say, "go on then, I'm up for it."

Commando sniggers and tells me not to rush straight in. I can see my two mates, being nosey and listening to our conversation. "I need to visit the loo, I'll be back" Commando says. He walks off and the other mate speaks

"A quality boxer, other coaches are already after you."

Seriously, I love all the positive comments! Before I get a bit too 'gassed', I ask Rezwan if he has finished sending the video. He replies, "Yeah you've received it." I reach out for my phone.

"Nope, you're not getting it back just yet."

"Why?" I ask, puzzled. He responds;

"Because Isaac Ingham, you have been a very naughty boy."

I'm so confused right now so I start to pay some attention.

"I wonder who Danielle . . . Dolton is?"

My face drops as he has finally found out.

"Why didn't you tell me you were going out with her? I'm your tightest boy G, and you kept it a secret. So now, I'm going to read the chat between you two and then you can have your phone back."

I nod representing 'oh god'. I should have told him however Rezwan has got a bit of a big mouth.

As for you my reader, now you have found out that I have a girlfriend. I had kept it a secret because it wasn't my intention to tell you however now you know though right?

Whilst still living the life of positive praise, Rezwan and my other mate, go through my phone. I am quite fed up now so I snatch my phone.

"Relax man! I've seen what I needed to" states Rezwan. "I'm hungry, lets go grab some munch, Peri Peri is just around the corner."

Carefully, I place my precious trophy into my gym bag ensuring that it is in a secure position. The three of us head towards the doors leading us outside. "Isaac! Where you going?" Shouts Commando.

My head immediately turns around.

"Going to grab some food Commando" I reply. After a few seconds he says,

"It better be healthy! And hurry up, we got to take pictures for the press and many people want to meet you" conveys Commando. I nod at him and smile. We carry on strolling, The Three Musketeers.

As we enter the shop, the boys dig deep in their pockets to reach out for money. At the same time, I grab their arms and say "this one's on me." They say thank you. After we order our food, Rezwan and I do a bit of light sparring in the shop; quite weird nevertheless it's minor. I teach him a few moves and skills. 5 minutes later, Rezwan walks over to Waseem (the other mate) and they begin to talk secretively. As soon as I walk over, they both stop talking. "What you lot's on about?" I question. They look at each other and then Waseem talks, "just gossiping"

"About?" I ask.

"Why the questions? It's just about school" speaks Rezwan. The both of them smirk and it is quite obvious that they're hiding something from me. Conversation slowly dies out as our food has come and the three of us munch like dogs. Gradually, we make our way back to the Arena where the show is taking place. My phone rings. "Hold my box" I say to Waseem as I hand it over. 'Mumzy!' reads my phone.

My mother is ringing me, I pick up.

"Hi mum"

"Hello son, how's the boxing?"

"Wicked! I won my fight!"

"That's fantastic; where are you now?"

"I went to get some food"

"What you eating? And are you alone?!"

"Standard chicken and chips; and of course not,

I'm with some mates from school"

"What are their names?"

"Why are you so suspicious?"

"I'm just making sure"

"Anyway, Commando will drop me off home around 11pm so see you soon"

"Take care son."

I hang up. Waseem passes me my box of chicken and chips back. I continue to munch. After we reach the venue, numerous strangers congratulate me once again for my win. We head at the back of the room and sit at the top row. I recognise the boxer that is fighting now. He boxes for Boxwell; his name is Robby. To me, he isn't a boxer. He Street fights whilst up there. No skill, just dull jabs and off-key hooks.

Surprisingly, his record is undefeated. Robby's never lost a fight. I wonder if he pays the judges to give him additional points.

I spot Commando a couple of rows below.

"Pass me your phone" asks Waseem. Without thinking, I give it.

"Unlock it then" he says.

I wipe my hands onto the tissue and type in the password.

"Safe" he speaks.

I notice him shuffling over to Rezwan. I get up and go to the toilet. As soon as I get back, I see Rezwan and Waseem looking happy, and I mean like, really happy. I approach them and ask why they're smiling. Coincidentally, a fit girl is sitting opposite them, which explains it. Waseem hands me back my phone and this is when I actually realise what they were doing on my phone all this time. I go on to BBM.

"Did you get the pic?xx" sends Danielle. I decide not to look at the two boys next to me right away because I don't want to accuse them.

"What pic?x" I reply.

"Previous messages baby xx" she responds back. I get very curious. I scroll up and click the option 'previous messages' and this is when I see the image. An irrelevant image sent by Danielle of something indecent. I get furious, so I ask Waseem and Rezwan if they got any answers to explain this nudity situation. "I asked her as a joke!" says Waseem.

"What the hell is wrong with you?!" I speak angrily.

"I didn't know your slag of a girlfriend would actually send it, did I?" He replies.

I take a few breaths and then laugh, "YOLO!"

I high five the two boys and tell them that it's cool as long as the picture doesn't go round. I examine the picture very, very closely. "Ooh, fiesty!" I convey immaturely. Rezwan and Waseem laugh uncontrollably. I remind the two lads not to tell anyone about the picture. They agree not too. The night continues with bouts and an interesting environment.

CHAPTER 11

Worst of all . . .

FREEZE! That night was one never to forget. Firstly, I won my fight, talked to the press and went on the newspaper. The second thing was the Danielle issue. However, it didn't go so straight forward. Things got awkward between Danielle and I. Due to us hardly speaking, her face expressed as if she was worried. Then the worst thing of all happened. My whole year had found out that I was going out with Danielle and that wasn't even the worst part. Many had found out that she sent me a picture of herself and it didn't take long before the news reached to her. As soon as I had found out (loads of people were coming up to me), I went to Waseem and Rezwan first. I told them if they had told anyone and Waseem said no, so did Rezwan. They were arguing accusing one another. I gave up and went to seek for Danielle. Her mates came up to me, shouting and screaming at me; "why'd you force her?!"

I was left clueless as I had no idea. I asked where Danielle was however her mates told me she was in the toilets crying her eyes out. Being part of a gang back in the days meant you're not allowed to snitch. That is why Danielle told her mother and her mum contacted the police. Ridiculously, I covered up for my boys and told the police that I did it. I got into a lot of trouble for this. My parents were contacted and the school investigated further. From that day, I had no contact with Danielle and remained a trouble-maker. Relating back to the story, due to this issue, it led me to get permanently excluded. This was the cause of leaving me with no hope in life. Anyway, after all the business that happened, I found out that Waseem stitched me up. Oh boy was I angry that day. He was eating his dinner and I had run up to him. I was swearing continuously and when I was finally about to hit him, my close mate Rezwan, jumped in the way. My off-key swing connected with Rezwans jaw which enabled him to fall to the ground. I was out of control, everyone was staring at me but I couldn't give two sh*ts. Rezwan got up and rugby tackled me. He told me to calm down and was holding me onto my seat. Waseem ran off. That day, I got into a little more trouble because of my stupid lash out. I got excluded for 3 days to calm down and have a break from school. Everyday, I was getting the most amounts of lectures from my parents that went through one ear and out the other. Finally, when I came back to school, I committed another incident, a fight. However this wasn't like an ordinary fight. This ended horrifically which allowed the teachers to kick me out on the spot due to the damage that happened to my challengers face. Want to hear the story from my view? Carry on . . .

I get uncomfortable looks from the students that walk past by me. Without talking to anyone, I walk towards my first lesson; dance. Casually, I get changed minding my own business. At length, a boy asks me a question "What happened with you and Danielle?" This makes me fumingly angry.

I turn around and go up close to him. Everyone is watching. I begin to raise my voice, "next person that talks about Danielle, I'll rip their heart out!" From then on, nobody talks to me, I got to say, it feels quite lonely. Girls give me disgusted looks whilst the boys daren't to look straight into my eyes. I hardly participate in the lesson and am relieved when lesson finishes. Then again, I walk into the changing rooms, minding my own business before someone interrupts. A boy walks in the changing rooms, a rather fat kid. I recognise him immediately as I have had a fight with him before.

He pats me on my back and says "You're back! I rate you man, you got a picture of Danielle. What a player!"

This is the part where I simply, go nuts! I grip on his school shirt and push him against the wall. I whisper "fight me now before I kill you in here."

Straight away, he kicks me directly onto my stomach. I get winded for several of seconds. My turn! I run into him, push him into the corner and use my elbows to demolish him. The lads watching in the room are shouting and cheering but their sounds are drained out. I am virtually ready to kill this guy. I am uncontrollable and I mean it. Someone grabs me off the kid and I punch the wall. This increases my aggressiveness and I run back at him for more. A straight jab connects with his face and before you know it, I resume jabbing, hooking and upper cutting this waste of skin. Everyone grabs hold of me this time and pushes me away.

I think I have done the job so I don't go back for more again. Everyone is surrounding the fat kid. Impatiently, I budge through. This is when I observe his face clearly. The sides of his face are turned to green-like bruises whilst the main damage is done beneath his right eye. He has his hands cuffed in a cupped motion allowing the squirts of blood to place inside. I am gobsmacked because this guy is bleeding really badly. He looks dazed. What shall I do? The boys look at me as I gather my belongings and hurriedly exit out.

My heart races rapidly. I stand outside the PE changing rooms. There's a notice on the door. 'NO PE. COME TO H12, YEAR 9!' After I read it, it gives me a thought. I run outside to the playground, and light up a snout. This makes me feel a little relaxed. I hear the middle corridor doors open. Straight away, I put it out, wait a couple of seconds and see Alex walk by. He looks at me and says "you look a little shocked"

I light the snout up again and tell him everything is fine. After the smoke, I head towards H12. What happened to the boy now? What are the consequences? Guilt runs through my veins. However one part of me tells me I have done the right thing. Think about the positives, how much rep will I receive? The Mayhem Crew will love me for this! My head is down as I enter the room. Even though I am not looking up, I can sense everyone looking at me. I lift my head to have a glimpse. I am right, the pupils in the class are looking on and off at me. I assume they found out; I guess the teachers will sooner or later find out. Thinking about this, reminds me to consider a few excuses. I won't 'lie' to them, I'll just say a 'white lie', and there are two different meanings to both contexts.

One of the boys that witnessed the fight, I noticed him recording. As soon as I establish that it was him, I ask him if I can see the video. "One sec . . . You destroyed him man, and I'm not sure if I should mention it but he got taken away by the assistant Head of Year." This blows me away, my heart begins to beat hastily and my palms begin to sweat. I try to remain calm and ask the boy if he snitched on me. "I ain't too sure but I did hear him saying that he just banged his eye onto the peg", I take in a gulp as I feel a little dehydrated. He passes me his phone and I watch the video.

I notice me banging this guy into the corner; demolishing him. My punches were splattering everywhere. As the crowd began to cheer, I muted the sound. The PE teacher is near the door so I remain watching the video. Afterwards, I see Waseem pulling me back. Stupidly, I run back into the fight to finish the boy off. Then again, I witness myself, knocking the boy down. After a few more rapid hits, I get dragged off by Waseem once again. The video cuts off.

"What the hell did I just do?" I say, loudly. Heads in the room turn to my direction. Then they start whispering. Due to the situation I'm in, I begin to recite a few prayers. 'Lord, please help me. I have committed a sin. Please forgive me and keep me out of trouble.'

Storming into the classroom is Ms Confield. "Get yourself out of this classroom right now!" she bellows, incredibly loudly. The class becomes deeply silent. I shiver with shock. How I'm feeling now, is the worst feeling I have ever experienced. I reach for my bag and quietly head out of the room with my head down. Outside the class are other two teachers. They are important to the school as they have a big role. This is major. This is game over. Ms Confield exits behind me, she looks FURIOUS. "You are pure filth; a disgraceful pupil to this school. You're a bully. I can't even look at you!" Ms Confield walks off, speedily walking down the corridor. Another teacher takes over, "Today you have done a very, very bad thing. You have harmed a pupil extremely . . . absolutely horrific; to get to the point, you assaulted another pupil, Louis Dames." Hearing his name, I raise my head and look the teacher in the eyes. I feel tears arising however I prevent them from dropping. "Follow me" orders the 'high-profiled' teacher. I amble behind dragging my bag. This is the time to think of an idea which I can portray to the teachers. As I already know that Louis told the teachers he banged his eye on the peg, I might as well adapt on that. This is a rough idea that I will say. 'All the boys were having a 'royal rumble' in the changing room and Louis was behind me. Whilst everyone was virtually killing each other, I tried to step back however I got caught up in the action. As I was also getting pushed, I slipped and gripped Louis for support but he slipped too and he banged his eye onto the peg.

I do plead guilty for making him slip however it was a definite 'accident.' That is what I will say and I will make something up on spot with the confrontation questions that I will have to answer. I hope I get away with this.

I enter an area that I have never been in before; it is where all the bigger classed department of teachers spend their school day, in their offices. I feel dreadful. This can be my last day in Moore's East Academy. I can feel the sweat bracing from my collar, "sit there" instructs the teacher. I take the seat and sit down. I slouch on the chair as if I couldn't give a damn. Then the worst possible teacher comes out of her office and talks to a few other teachers. Witnessing her hand coordinates which are pointing at me including her facial expressions, I clock on that the group of teachers are explaining why I am here.

This isn't the first time she met me, on other several occasions, I was sent to her due to my disruptive behaviour. Her name is Miss Borich. She walks past me and says "you are terrible. This school has given you many chances and this is probably the last one. Sorry to say but after what I've heard, you're outta here mate" I still couldn't give a monkeys. I am as cool as a cucumber and even though I am a little terrified of the consequences, I try to maintain a clam approach. "There's a statement sheet and be honest. When I read the first sentence and it doesn't match another witness account, I'm ripping it straight up." Miss Borich conveys. I answer her back, "who said I'm going to lie, I didn't know you were psychic." She gives me a daring look and responds "enough of the cheek and get writing" bravely I reply back again, "who said I want to write. My hand hurts so I can't be bothered." I can see her temper rising. "I'll get on with it if I were you because you're in a very sticky situation." I remain slouched in my seat. Even though I'm not in the mood, I begin to write, a statement with false information however they do not know that. The plan I thought of before, I include it onto the paper.

After completing the sham statement, I hand it over to Miss Borich without making any contact.

"This is the truth right?" she asks. I remain silent as I do not want to speak to her. "I'm trying to persuade you to do the right here so is this the truth?" she repeats. I roll my eyes toward her and bluntly say yes. She tells me that she thinks its all lies. I say again that it is not and it's the truth. She walks back into her office and read the statement. I feel a little shook up. A few minutes later, my Head of Year enters, Ms Confield with a couple lads behind her. Instantly, I recognise them as they were in the changing rooms at the time the incident took place.

Ms Confield allocates the other boys to sit in different parts of the room. Each one that walks by, I give an extensive. Somehow I try to communicate with them by looking into their eyes, hoping they can read my mind; 'you didn't snitch did you?!'; Ms Confield shouts "look down and don't speak to them!" she irritates me so aggressively, the response I give back is "did you see my mouth moving?! If not, go get your eyes tested!"

All eyes turn to my direction.

"You need to watch what you're saying. You're in enough trouble as it is! Louis is in A&E right now, getting his face checked and you're the one that caused it! You've sent a student in your year to Hospital and you still think it's acceptable to talk to a member of staff like that, don't you?" Ms Confield bellows.

That totally knocked me down; Louis is in Hospital. Did I damage him that badly? This time, I don't respond and look down. She hands a pen and a statement sheet to the other kids. Trying to convey a message to the rest, I cough and say 'don't snitch'. Due to the obviousness, Ms Confield orders, "get in that room behind you and keep the door closed so no-one can see your face." Disturbingly, I slam my seat in and grab my bag; following that, I try to create a loud noise by slamming the door. I hear Miss Borwich saying "He's definitely out of this school." Finally, some sense knocks into my head and I begin to think of the consequences. What will my parents think? What if they kick me out of the house? Where will I go? During the rest of the period I remain silent. I twiddle my thumbs for 30 minutes straight till I spot Louis. Within a second, I get up and observe his face. The left side was covered in bruises and the other had an ice pack onto it. As he rotated his head, he spotted me. He stepped back a couple of steps. His has a black eye and a plaster on the bottom of his right eye. I noticed his father is with him. I expect his Dad to budge through to the room I am sat, and to beat to crap out of me. Luckily that hasn't happened, yet. They both enter Miss Borich's office and talk.

I sit back down with my hands on my head. Guilt overtakes me.

CHAPTER 12

The Last Days

FREEZE! *That day, I got excluded for a fixed 5 days which can lead to a permanent exclusion; so the Academy can do further investigation within the incident, Hope is what I relied on. The amount of pain and shock my parents suffered, was unbelievable. I prayed a lot during the 5 days and tried to study as much as possible. No positives were coming to my head except the negative ones. Even though I didn't want to think about it, I knew that I was going to get expelled. On the 6th day, I had to go in for a meeting due to what was going to happen to me now and what consequences I will have to face with. This is what happened during the meeting with my parents . . .*

My parents are too upset to even talk or look at me however even if they physically didn't show me, I know that they are breaking to pieces inside. We park outside the school and we walk in. My parents go up to the Receptionist, "we're here to have a meeting with Miss Borich."

Unnoticeably, I stand behind. "She'll be out here in a couple of minutes, please take a seat" answers the Receptionist. I see a mate and handshake them. "Why aren't you in school?" asks a mate of mine. "I got kicked out and now having a meeting" I reply. My mum calls me over so I handshake him again and say bye. I notice my mum staring at the boy as he is exiting the school; I can sense that she is trying to judge his character. Quietly, I sit down. 3 minutes later, Miss Borich turns up; she speaks, "sorry for the lateness, I had another meeting with another pupil, please follow me."

My parents and I walk into the area where all the 'high-classed teachers' offices are. Just as I am about to enter Miss Borich's office, Miss notifies my parents that I am not allowed in the room whilst the meeting is taking place. This upsets me as I will have to wait for the final decision even longer. I sit down in a chair nearby the office. "Take a seat" says Miss Borich and then she shuts the door giving me the 'why did you do it?' look. I look down and stare at the grey carpet. As I have no clue what they are discussing, I begin to ask God if he will help me. My mother turns around and instantly I make eye contact with her. Unfortunately, she isn't looking too happy.

This is when I begin to feel like crap. What did I do and why did I do it? They are the only two questions clouding my head. I begin to hear my father's voice, slowly starting to rise. I cannot make out what he is saying as the sound is not clear.

45 minutes later, the meeting comes to an end. I stand up straight away and see my mother carrying a few documents. My parents look as if they are about to cry and I knew it isn't going to be good news. "Isaac, unfortunately our final decision is if you go to, not a high school but for the time-being, if you go to a training college. We are sorry for the decision we concluded therefore you will no longer be a member of our school."

Well, that is it. No more of Moore's East Academy, it is all over. I handshake both principals and say sorry and then thank them for giving me chances. We walk out of the building. My father speaks "Look up, this is your final time seeing the schools name. You've left your sister to go to this school without you being there. Have you realised what you have done?!"

When he turns around, I unhurriedly look behind and mutter "sorry."

CHAPTER 13

Expressing Me

FREEZE! Well I guess it was all over; time to settle somewhere else. The feelings I felt were unexplainable however, how will you be feeling if you got kicked out of high school? Take some time to think about it . . . how will your parents feel? What emotions will you go through? Whatever you're thinking about is exactly how I felt at the time. Nonetheless, after a week of misery, I had a meeting with the training college. The kids, were young adults and much older than me. I did feel a little unsecure. After the confirmation was made, I started attending. Surprisingly, the timetable was nothing like a high-school day. The day would begin at 10am till 4pm. A few hours of extra sleep, I liked. Monday—ICT, Tuesday—PSHE (behaviour etc), Wednesday—Working in an office environment, this was the opportunity to work in an office with adults, Thursday—Whole day of Functional Skill Mathematics and Friday—English. I enjoyed being here. The students and workers were incredibly friendly and welcoming. Everyday, my mother would go up to the 'School Placement' department to find me a space in a school.

However, going back to the training college, I had found out that they were also another company 'Community Needs'. Referring to the organisation name, you probably figured out what they do. A bunch of volunteer's age form 16-30+ help different wards around Luton, such as: family fun days, ESOL courses, ICT courses and many, many more. This took my interest and I asked the Manager, M. Igor and he said to create leaflets for their upcoming events. Slowly, I got closer and closer to becoming a member of the organisation. Eventually, after a month of helping out here and there, I was allocated to help out on one of their events. My parents were proud of me and to see them smile after an awfully long time, I was proud. The company helped me strive towards success and without the support of M. Igor and the Chairperson of the organisation, Sadiqul, I wouldn't have got where I am now. Sadiqul once told me 'Sometimes You Have To Make Sacrifices In Life', He was referring to boxing; I was no longer allowed to do it as I was banned from the club. It was incredibly hard to give it up as I gave most of my time up for it however I accepted the quote after a long period. When I thought everything was going fantastic, I made one of the biggest mistakes I have ever done; I smoked an illegal drug. I won't go in depth as it affects me emotionally as it nearly took my life. My parents started back from square one with their trust for me. Because of this action, I was kicked out of the 'training college' too. After a long persuasive talk my Father had with the M. Igor, he decided to take me on again. Things got awkward as the whole department knew what happened. Gradually, things started to pick up again; I resumed going swimming with my 'older' mates from the company and did a lot of activities with them. I also continued helping out with events and met many people. This was 4 months in when I got kicked out from Moore's.

For the next 2 months, I did something no other kid my age had done. Community Needs held a programme called 'The Apprentice', very similar to the TV show. Bravely, I nominated myself to be a Project Manager. We started off with 11 teams as there were 11 Project Managers (PM's). Business is no experience that I, and a few other PM's had, so I definitely knew it was going to be a challenge, our group was called Inception.

Gradually, PM's got fired and their team members were allocated into different groups as well as the ex PM. It was surprising how our group still wasn't fired however I had an advantage, Sadiqul was in my group throughout. After a long 2 months of advertising, leafleting and collecting sponsorship money, there were 3 groups left; an 18 year old (Shavir), a 16 year old (Claire) and myself, aged 13. All the members found it hard to take in as in how is it possible for a 13 year old to get this far. For me too, it was quite shocking. After everything was settled, we were told what we were going to do. We were allowed to hold many events as we wanted and had to make income out of it however it wasn't about which group makes the most profit, 30% accounted towards profit and the other 70% accounted for, creativity, attitude, problem-solving, time management etc. Besides from all the side events we held, there was one main one each group had to hold; a fun day at a local Primary School. Fortunately, our day went really good. The little kids enjoyed it. After all the events were over, we were told the company will hold an award ceremony where all the presentation and rewards will be presented alongside the winner of the Apprentice.

Anyways, I was now knocking myself back on track which was an awesome thing to do. I miss my mates from Moore's so, so much. However reality has to hit at some point which makes you realise. Imagine, your mates, the ones you grew up with; one day, you stopped seeing them. No bye, no tears, you just disappear. They'll be wondering and you're distressed when you reflect on memories. We feel the pressure when one of our mates departs. I didn't leave one, two or three mates behind. I left the majority of Moore's behind. These were the people I spent most of my time with and spent growing up with them. Well, life takes you in different directions nevertheless, seek for the positives.

Summer holidays went promptly due to the Apprentice taking up most of the time. Unluckily, I still wasn't sure if I would be going back to high school any sooner. Then a phone call came notifying my parents and I that I have a chance to go back to Moore's East. Words cannot be conveyed on how delighted I was. My parents seemed relieved however I don't think they wanted me to go back but I didn't really have a choice. I noticed my parents smiles were gradually staying on their faces. Except, two days later, Miss Borich gets in contact and gives the worst possible news; I am not allowed back into the school and still need to seek for another one; false hope.

As students/parents were heading towards their first days back into school/work, I was left at home, depressed. After a long week, another phone call came through to my house. "Your son will be going to Ashford High School starting from the new week." Then again, I was over the moon. Surprisingly, another phone call got in contact informing us that I have been given a space at another school 'Dunkell's High School', the best in our Borough.

I knew many people that go to this school; majority were Muslims. Referring to high school students, they don't really comprehend that whatever they do in High school; most of it will be forgotten in the future. They act as if they know the right and wrongs however they haven't got a clue what the future holds for them.

CHAPTER 14

Dunkell's High School

"You've got another chance after a long time. You put yourself through a lot and us too. This is classed as the Best School so put your head down. Whatever's in the past stays there, focus on the present. I want you to prove to Moore's High that they made the wrong decision of excluding you, show them who you really are, the changed you. Good luck son and think before you speak as well as your actions." My dad gives the last minute explanation in the car. My face is covered with a smile. I am feeling a little nervy; I haven't been to school in 8 months. The uniform I have on now, makes me feel proud; a new school with different teachers and students. I know that I won't repeat my mistakes. I stare at the window and experience many feelings, emotional mainly. I have been to this school a few times during the holidays. The school is very old and big. Estimating, there is 3 minutes left till I enter Dunkell's High School.

"Shall I walk you in?" asks Dad.
"No! I'll go by myself, don't worry" I counter.

I take in a deep breath and open the door. My Dad says good luck once again and I close my eyes and step outside. I rotate my head around and I witness a few heads already looking at me. There is a teacher outside the gates and she asks me my name. "Are you new to the school?" she questions.

"Yes Miss, I am." I reply.

She asks, "Do you need someone to take you in?"

I smile and respond "Don't worry, I'll find my way."

I turn my head and see my Dad staring out from the car window. I wave at him and he waves back. I carry on walking. It didn't even take a matter of seconds before a whole bunch of students come up to me and ask "Are you the new boy?!"

"Erm . . . Yeah I am"

Many came up to ask, I presume they're in my year. I try to spot the 'fit' girls however I haven't come across any just yet. A few feet in front of me, I see a bunch of lads staring at me. "Yo! You're here Bro!" speaks Rashid excitedly.

"What you saying g?" I reply.

I give those manly hugs/handshakes.

"Those lots in our year?" I ask referring to the boys across me.

"Yeah, I think they starting to cause beef" Rashid replies.

I start to walk to them, Rashid follows.

"Safe, you lots in my year yeah?" I convey.

It took a little time to notice that I am actually trapped in a circle and the lads are around me. "Who said this is YOUR year?" says this 'tall' kid.

I snigger and speak "Oh, that came out wrong. Are you in year 9?"

He replies "Yeah"

I counter "Bloody hell you're tall!"

He is like double the height of me.

"Catch you lot in a bit" I walk off and ask Rashid who's the roughest out of them.

"PUSSY!" Shouts a person behind us, it is from the lads in year 9. I halt and tell Rashid I'm going back to them to sort it out. "Relax man, it's your first day" he explains.

I stare at the lads and spit on the floor. I carry on strolling around with Rashid.

I look into my planner and ask Rashid to take me to that specific room. "Take me here, it's my form room" I order.

"It next door to mine, let's go" he says.

It feels quite awkward as people just stare. I observe the students and the building itself. This is nothing compared to Moore's £30 million new built school. Dunkill's is ancient. However, it isn't about how to school looks, it is about the teaching and education.

FREEZE! Going back to school after a long amount of time, was relieving. Simply, I was in high spirits. Everyone gave a warm welcoming except a few jealous students. Before you knew it, I was in classes, learning. Losing out on Education is fatal. You see those males/females in their German cars and rich suits; well they studied hard and focussed on their futures. Each individual wants to be like them however in order for that to become real, you've got to learn, you have to study. Keep in mind that most of your time is freedom; you have to be committed to give minimum 10 years away to learning and studying. Give up the mischief you cause and merely, realise. Life takes you in many directions but the decision lies with you in which path you want to end up in. Dunkill's was the best school to be in, students to improve is what each teacher always keeps in mind.

2 months in Dunkill's, the Community Needs ceremony was around the corner. I remember the tension between the three groups. This was how the evening turned out.

I ask my mother to iron my blazer as well as my shirt whilst I have a shower. As I hand over my garments, I ask her "who will be going?"

She replies "Dad will come later but your little brother and I will come."

I smile and head towards the bathroom. As I walk past the living room, my sister speaks,

"Good luck loser."

"Thanks? It's going to be awesome man; you're missing out on my rap about Community Needs" I reply.

"You're actually going to rap; you're going to make a fool out of yourself" she explains.

"Relax, I've got this. I've had plenty of practice." I counter.

"Tell Mum to record it" she utters.

After I have the shower, I come back upstairs and collect my clothes from my parent's room and walk back to mine to get changed. I play a song out loud called 'Hall Of Fame' as I dramatically get changed as if it's my wedding day. After I get ready, as usual, I take a quick snap of myself; we call it a 'Selfie'. My mother rings my father and tells him to make his way. As I head downstairs, my sister repeats good luck again and heads up the stairs. "Make sure you don't open the door when someone you don't know knocks" my mum says to my sister. "I'm not 6 any more, don't you worry."

My mum, younger brother and I get into the car. The venue is local so it won't take us that long. Evening is due so the time is now, 6:52pm; the ceremony will start at 7pm. Eventually, when we get there, I handshake the male members and register the family and myself in. We take our seat and I pick up the leaflet of the time management and when everything will happen. As I scroll down with my eyes to look for my name, I spot at 9:00pm, I will be on stage. Food will be served at 8pm so I will be on after we have eaten. I point it out to my mum and she says "don't worry; I've got the camcorder ready."

***FREEZE!** The ceremony kicked off with two funny hosts, Simon and Stewart. They go through each slide about what events we had held and what charities we raised money for. After the presentation, all the members of Community Needs were brought up on stage to collect a certificate for their work and participation. Nerves were slowly building up as my performance was coming up . . . I will skip to the rapping scene.*

I get on stage and the instrumental begins to play. I feel the flow and notice myself feeling the beat. I spot my dad smiling and my mum with the camcorder. Loads are just staring at me. I begin to rap:

*'First mistake was when I went straight in for the wack,
didn't even think about looking back,
One smack in his eye, that's it, he was flat.*

(I refer to the part when I had the fight in the Dance Changing Rooms.)

Now I think I've learnt it,
Definitely earned it.
I've tried so hard,
Didn't wanna throw in the towel,
First time, it was a dirty foul.
But no more, I was immature then,
I won't repeat the mistakes again.
(I express, saying that I have learnt from what mistakes I have done and that now, all the sins I had committed have been replaced by my good deeds)

Sadiqul said 'Sometimes you have to make sacrifices in life, to be on top'
He told me why I should stop,
Now I found out this was a big flop,
Get them out of the picture, simply press crop.
(In the third verse, I mention Sadiqul's quote and he told me to leave the bad crowd. Realising too late, ended up me dealing with the consequences)

CN, thank you for everything,
You helped me to get my life back on track,
Every step I took, you had my back.
I really want to thank you for that.
(This is the chorus CN is short for Community Needs in case you didn't notice. Also, I convey how CN helped me reach the top and supported me)

I was asleep, dreaming deep.
I knew I had Community Needs,
They were there for me, wanted me to succeed,
So when I'm older, I'll be the one to lead.
I just wanna gather up my good deeds.
Count them up, stack them up,
Before, I used to be so messed up.
Could do anything, drink from the queen's cup.
(CN were there for me and I portray positives, and at this point, I also 'big' myself up a little.)

I met many learning curves,
Before, I didn't have any nerves,
I got everything I deserved.
But lord help me, I don't wanna face that path again,
Before I was so insane, didn't think I had a brain.
(I made the mistakes due to my insane stupidity and I hope I never go down the route again)

Did the most dumbest things, its unthinkable,
I thought I was unsinkable, but I was wrong.
Banging on my chest like King Kong,
That's why I put together this song,
Wanted to make so long.
(Made the incorrect choices, thought I was invincible)

CN, thank you for everything,
You helped me to get my life back on track,
Every step I took, you had my back. I really want to thank you for that.

(Chorus once again)

Couldn't have done it without you lot,
You put the right slot in the right plot,
This made me think before the blink,
How much I learnt, how much I've earned.
(They directed me to do things the correct way and made me realise reality)

Shavir said 'Everything that happens, happens for the best,
You've got to realise that life is a test,
Head down man, forget about the rest,
My life used to be a mess.
(Shavir introduced me into CN, and he told me that quote. You need to think positive and he got that message across to me.)

A round of applause went around the hall and I felt relieved after coming down the stage steps. As I walk back to my seat, a few of the members congratulate me. "Well done, I've recorded it and now eat some food" praises mum. My little brother gives me a high five. Due to the nervousness, I couldn't eat however, as my plate is full up with Kebabs, Rice, Chicken Tikka, I munch like crazy.

After a few more members perform their individual talent, the awards/rewards time is here. They start off in different categories e.g. Commitment award, Dedication Award, Exceptional Award, One in a Million award. The members nominated each other for which category suited them best. Many members are collecting awards and taking pictures; I am anxious if I will get one or not. With all my hard work, I do hope I get one. Just as I am thinking about it, I get the Runner-up for the Exceptional Award. I go up on stage to collect it. Loads of other mini rewards are handed out to the employees however each member is keen on the Apprentice Shield, who will win? Personally, I don't think we do have a chance because we made many mistakes however we tried our best to repair them. Also, I caught chicken pox during the Apprentice month and things began to collapse nevertheless, you never know; we may still have a chance. I'm presuming Shavir's group is going to win; he is experienced in this type of stuff. Anyway, we'll wait and see. 10 minutes later, M. Igor announces "now for the time we've all been waiting for. Who has won the Apprentice 2014?"

Curiously, everyone listens. I sit next to my group members, feeling nervous and excited. "We've got this" I murmur to the members sitting around the table. "Isaac, would you like to collect your shield?" Just I am about to get up happily, a member of my team drags me down. "He is trying to trick you!" he publicises. A few laugh and I announce, "You almost got me but you didn't."

"Drum role please" asks M. Igor to the audience. We all begin to bang on the table, repeatedly.

"Enough, enough . . . and the winner is TEAM INCEPTION!"

We won! We actually pulled it off! Absolutely unbelievable! Each of our team members stand up and head towards the stage, we all hug/handshake one another and walk; a moment to be proud.

Many cheer and clap. I walk passed Shavir and pat him on his back "Good try mate, you've still got next year."

He didn't look too happy. As we get up on stage, I get into the middle, and claim the 2014 CN Apprentice Shield. Aged 13 and managed Business Project; wonderful.

FREEZE! Anyhow, after all the mistakes I made and amount of loss in Education in Year 8, I still managed to do my GCSE's by studying solidly. I was proud with the grades I got; 2 A*, 5 A's and 2 B's. I went to Sixth Form and continued to study, obviously with numerous silly mistakes.

Who doesn't make mistakes? We're all human aren't we? No mistakes, then where are the memories for us to remember?

Back to the Educational side of things; I completed 2 hard years of college and left with 2 A's and 1 B. Since Year 8, I knew what I wanted to become however I didn't want to express it to the public.

An Airline Pilot was the dream I always wanted to achieve to grow to be so I applied to go to a Pilot School out of Bedfordshire leading to learning the skills for the job.

Flying is the best thing for me, I feel free; the term 'You Only Live Once', stuck with me.

I dreamed and chased it; even if you 'flop', There's always Hope. Even in the worst case scenario, seek for the affirmatives. This can be for any reason e.g. if you're homeless, if you're kids are giving you headaches, also if you're getting bullied. Hope relates to every possible situation; believe that you can do it. In Year 8, I acknowledged failure and gave up. It did take a bit of time to realise that there is always a way, it's up to you whether you are willing to make the alteration.

I exceeded in life even making the mistakes and incorrect decisions however do not make misled conclusions. Why be a follower? Why not a leader? Think before you act, think about the consequences; you may not realise how much loss you actually create. I still felt the feelings when I was in Dunkill's. That emotion was, why did I do it? I grew up with the people in Moore's and suddenly let them go. Sensations affected me. It was my entire fault; I apologize for what I had done. The reason being, because I didn't think about the consequences; you may be the 'big boy' in your 'ends' but where will that get you in life? Imagine the future, not the present. Consider the positives, block the negatives. In addition, would you like to see a mate of yours, going down a steep slope of failure? Instead, help them up, enable them to realise. Distract them from bad. You are the change.

Unfortunately, my book is almost up to an ending; to conclude, I'd like to leave you with a little quote.

'Hope you will achieve, stick to the dedication, believe the commitment, State to attain as success is the aim.

Practise the things that are worth practising for. An individual is special in their own way, make use.
Believe, Achieve, And Succeed.'

Lightning Source UK Ltd.
Milton Keynes UK
UKOW02f0753280914

239284UK00002B/48/P